Involving Students in Questioning

Involving Students in Questioning

Francis P. Hunkins
University of Washington
Seattle

Allyn and Bacon, Inc.
Boston   London   Sydney

LIBRARY OF CONGRESS CATALOGING IN PUBLICATION DATA

Hunkins, Francis P
    Involving students in questioning.

    Bibliography: p.
    Includes index.
    1. Questioning. I. Title.
LB1027.H849   371.3'7   75-22294

ISBN 0-205-04866-8
Second printing ... June, 1977

To Leah,
Francis, Jr.,
Paul Stephen,
and Cheryl Ann

Contents

Foreword

Events within the last decade have dramatically indicated
that we live in a world society and that the social, economic,
and political problems that the world faces are tremendous.
Political alienation, inflation, energy scarcity, and pollution
are some of our serious international problems. Effective
solutions to these momentous problems can be found only
by an active and informed citizenry capable of making sound
public and private decisions that will benefit the world community. It is imperative for the school to play a decisive role
in educating citizens capable of functioning actively and effectively within the world society.

   To train reflective and totally active world citizens, many
of our traditional educational practices must be seriously
questioned and novel approaches, based on new assumptions,
must be implemented. Traditional educational practices emphasize student passivity and assume that the teacher is the
omniscient giver of truth and knowledge, and that the student is the inactive recipient of information and ideologies.
These kinds of practices, which are inconsistent with the

goals of a modern world society, are authoritarian, and tend to foster political apathy, inaction, intellectual stagnation, and indoctrination. Authoritarian educational approaches also promote a kind of insidious ethnocentrism and a provincial outlook which is antithetical to the development of what Lester Brown has insightfully called a "world without borders."

The demands of the final decades of this century dictate that we educate a new kind of citizen who is active rather than passive, who seriously questions rather than passively accepts, who is politically active rather than passive, and who is cosmopolitan rather than ethnocentric and culturally encapsulated. Planet Earth and its inhabitants will be seriously imperiled if the various peoples who inhabit it do not cooperatively solve their momentous problems within the next few decades.

This leads me to the importance of this significant and timely book. One of the basic assumptions underlying it is that students must be actively involved in their learning and that the teacher's major role is to arrange the learning environment in ways that will facilitate student learning. This assumption, and the techniques lucidly described by Professor Hunkins, will help teachers to educate students for active societal participation and for functioning effectively within the world society. Students who have the skill and commitment to question themselves, their leaders, and the basic assumptions of social and political systems are more likely, as adults, to be able to find viable solutions to the world's pressing problems since the questions we ask profoundly influence our conclusions and actions.

This book has several distinguishing characteristics which make it especially noteworthy. The author clearly describes many helpful strategies for involving students in questioning which the teacher can readily adapt for classroom use. This book should be enthusiastically received by teachers since they are always looking for insightful books that illustrate

how to translate theory into practice. The author successfully and effectively blends educational theory with specific
examples of how to implement it in the classroom setting.
Professor Hunkins was able to achieve this admirable balance
in the book because he is both a seasoned researcher on questioning techniques and a gifted teacher and writer.

This book is extremely timely and valuable because it
describes ways in which the teacher can help the student to
become a more active and reflective learner, and thus more
likely as an adult to contribute to the resolution of the enor-
mous problems which we face in the world community.
Teachers who can skillfully function in the role envisioned by
Professor Hunkins will greatly contribute to the improvement
of the human condition and to the salvation of Planet Earth.

James A. Banks
University of Washington
Seattle

Preface

"How do I get my students involved with questions and understanding process?" This is a question frequently posed by people involved in teaching. *Involving Students in Questioning* is a response to this question and attempts to provide teachers with practical suggestions for involving students at any level of education in planning, using, and assessing questions.

This book's entire thrust centers on the importance of student involvement and the centrality of questions to that involvement. Today, education continues to stress the active student, the involved student, the independent student. Education also advocates that the teacher assume the role of facilitator of student functioning both inside and outside of the classroom. The activities advanced in this book should assist the teacher to become a more effective facilitator of student learning. They should provide concrete examples of ways to get students involved in their own learning.

It should be stressed that this is a book for all prospective teachers and in-service teachers at all levels of education. Indeed, anyone interested in education in general and questions in particular should find it interesting and helpful.

The first chapter delineates the purpose of this book and provides background relating to student involvement. Chapter 2 deals with questions at the cognitive level, and chapter 3 discusses questions at the affective level. In chapters 2 and 3 numerous examples of questions at all levels in both domains are presented as well as key words to assist one in recognizing and planning questions at these various levels.

The major thrust of this book is on specific activities designed to assist the teacher in involving students in planning questions (chapter 4); in actually utilizing questions in various activities with particular strategies (chapter 5); and in assessing the effectiveness of their questions and others' questions and questioning strategies (chapter 6). Each of these three chapters presents numerous activities with emphasis on the basic rationale for each activity, a description of each activity, often with a sample sheet, a specific example of the activity in use in some curriculum area and grade level, and any other information pertinent to the activity. Many of the suggestions included in these three chapters have been tried out in classrooms by teachers who have participated in questioning strategies workshops. The last chapter (chapter 7) relates questions to models of teaching and to several modes of discovery.

In writing a book, one is influenced by many persons in a myriad of ways. I wish to thank my colleagues and friends in education both at the University of Washington and at other institutions who have provided me numerous opportunities for productive dialogue relating to teaching and questions. I thank all those publishers who granted me permission to quote or paraphrase selections from their books. I also wish to thank those individuals at Allyn and Bacon who provided guidance during the writing and production of the manuscript. Special thanks go to Mr. John Gilman who worked with me in the initial stages of this book and to Mr. Robert M. Roen who gave expert guidance during the total writing effort. I express my appreciation to those persons who reviewed the book and provided valuable suggestions: Dr. J. D. McAulay, Dr. Glen Fardig, Dr. John J. Carney and Dr. Drew Tinsley.

To my wife Doreen, I extend special thanks for her encouragement and cooperation as typist, proofreader, and idea catalyst. My children, Leah and Francis, assisted by being understanding and allowing me to work uninterrupted.

F.P.H.

Introduction

Teachers and students, the main actors in the current educational drama, are striving for meaningful involvement.
Meaningful involvement calls for teachers to create learning
encounters with the potential to get students excited about
and successful in their learning. It means educators functioning as designers of learning situations. It means being
innovative in our activities and in our strategies. It means
being "up front" in motivating students to consider particular learnings. It means being creative in meeting students'
needs and indeed creative in developing students' needs.

For students, meaningful involvement demands "hands
on" involvement with their learning. It means exploring and
delving into data. It means being involved in their learning,
seeing the relevance and payoff of learning. It means being
active in their learning, possessing the means and processes
for interacting with their environments both inside and
outside the school.

Today, educators are striving to be more effective facili-
tators of student learning. We are working at becoming in-

creasingly skilled in managing the educational scene in order to meet the diverse needs of students as defined by teachers, students and the wider society. We are constantly asking ourselves how we can design optimal learning environments. "How can I make this information meaningful to my students? How can I get the students to process the information in effective ways? How can this topic be made relevant? How can I assist my class in applying conclusions derived in one situation to another similar situation? How can I create a classroom atmosphere that will turn on kids?"

We are all posing these questions, and for various reasons. Some realize that we need to be innovative in involving students if we are to keep our clients interested in our efforts. Some of us are concerned with these questions for we not only wish to keep our clients, but we realize that the world needs individuals capable of participating at rational and moral or humanistic levels.

The world needs individuals who are not only autonomous, but who are humane. We teachers have the privilege and the challenge to provide students with opportunities to become rational, humane, and active persons. The profession of education is asking that we meet this challenge; society is requesting that we attend to this task. Students are demanding that we provide increased opportunities for them to "do their thing."

This demand for involvement and competent action by students in society requires precision in our fucntioning as educators. No guesswork will suffice if we are to meet the challenges. The public wants active students, and the students demand that we allow them to be active in their learning. In large measure we have already made great strides in meeting the demands of the profession, society, and the students. But we cannot relax our efforts in developing means of involving students in their learning.

Central to anyone's involvement in learning are the strategies used for processing data and arriving at warranted and meaningful conclusions. The learner does not arrive at

conclusions by accident or guesswork. Meaningful educational involvement only comes to those who work at it and
work at it systematically. Students will not become active
learners unless they are provided with opportunities for becoming involved in their learning and situations in which they
can obtain skills necessary for successfully functioning in
their learning. Students need to comprehend what is meant
by process learning, just as we teachers need to know.

⌐   The question is an integral, if not the integral, component
└in processing information. Regardless of whether a teacher is
functioning inductively or deductively with data, he or she
needs to generate questions. And the questions that are created and the manner in which they are phrased and
sequenced influences the quality, the significance, and the
accuracy of the learner's conclusions and what is done with
those conclusions.

     Since the question is so central to meaningful involve-
ment in learning, teachers need to be effective exemplars of
good questioners, and we need to provide students with formal and informal situations in which they can learn about the
realm of questions and questioning. We need to provide students with environments in which they can cognitively confront and affectively consider their questions and the
questions of others.

     The question and questioning strategies are not simple to
understand. It takes time to learn the many dimensions of
questions. It takes time to uncover the numerous strategies
in existence and the roles of questions in them. But it is time
well spent for it will provide understanding that will be useful
throughout the students' lives.

     In essence, this book provides input which will enable in-
service teachers and prospective teachers to assist students in
becoming knowledgeable and skilled with queries and strategies of which questions are integral components. This book,
hopefully, will increase our commitment to the active student. It should assist us in designing and providing situations
and activities in which students can plan their questions and

strategies, carry out their plans, and assess their effectiveness in utilizing strategies. Additionally, it should allow students to be critical processors and consumers of information that has been produced by others. This book should assist teachers in setting the educational stage for effective student questions and questioning.

1

Getting Students Involved

> In the skillful use of the question more than in anything else lies the fine art of teaching; for in such use we have the guide to clear and vivid ideas, the quick spur to imagination, the stimulus to thought, the incentive to action.[1]

This book responds to the teacher's question: How do I get my students involved with questions, with understanding process? by providing some practical suggestions for student involvement in three aspects of information processing: the planning stage, the doing stage, and the assessing stage. Learners need to be involved in planning their questions and led to realize the myriad ways to plan. They also need to comprehend the numerous models available for processing information. Some of these models relate to obtaining a better understanding of information, others relate to attaining a better understanding of process, while some relate to acquiring a more complete understanding of self. Students

1

also need to learn procedures for assessing the effectiveness of their questioning procedures.

This book aims at pointing out to teachers, prospective teachers, and eventually students that the question is of paramount importance to all process models. Without the question there is no processing of information. The absence of the question indicates an absence of learning, for it is the question that centers the person's attention upon some topic; it is the question that enables data processing; and it is the question that determines whether a conclusion is justified or not.

This book should exemplify, through the numerous activities discussed, the dependence of learning quality upon question quality. Learners using knowledge questions will obtain information relating to fact, and learners posing analysis questions centering on basic assumptions will derive insights into those assumptions. But learners skilled only in formulating knowledge questions who are eager to be able to identify assumptions will fail to achieve their objective. This book should provide ways for the teacher to reduce the incidence of failure among students.

Although intended for in-service and prospective teachers, this is not a book to provide means for improving teacher questions, teacher question planning, or teacher question strategies, although it should help. A book for that specific purpose is *Questioning Strategies and Techniques.*[2] This current text focuses on what the teacher can do to elicit student action. By following the suggestions in this book, teachers hopefully will be able to make students the primary performers in the classroom.

The activities indicated in this textbook should provide students with the means to become independent learners, but teachers must first accept some basic premises for this to occur. Perhaps the major assumption is one expounded by Rogers in his book on *Client Centered Therapy:*

> You can trust the student. You can trust him to desire to
> learn in certain ways which will maintain or enhance the

self; you can trust him to make use of resources which will serve this end; you can trust him to evaluate himself in ways which will make for self-progress; you can trust him to grow, provided the atmosphere for growth is available to him.[3]

Certainly, if the teacher is to engage his or her students in the activities suggested within this text then he or she must believe that students can plan much of their approach to processing information, that they can execute their plans, and that they can assess the effectiveness of their actions.

Another premise central to this book is the cruciality of students' involvement in educational encounters if the students are to develop skills in processing information, whether inductively or deductively. As pointed out by Carin and Sund,[4] a growing body of research exists which indicates that students attain higher levels of thinking when encouraged to develop skill in asking their own questions and when provided with more opportunities for dialogue with classmates about the questions posed and conclusions derived from information. The activities in this book suggest ways in which we as teachers can furnish students with opportunities for enhancing their questions and question asking and for engaging in meaningful interaction with their fellow learners. Carin and Sund note that providing activities for involving students in student-student interaction has the following virtues:

1 Tends to produce more sustained variety and enriched responses both from individuals and from a greater variety of children.

2 Stimulates volunteering by more students.

3 Contributes to more group cooperation.

4 Approaches a more realistic social situation.

5 Minimizes the tendency toward teacher-dominated lessons.

6 Places burden for *active* learning upon student rather than over-dependence upon teacher.

7. Increases flow of ideas and avoids fragmenting discussion.[5]

4 *Getting Students Involved*

BASIC RATIONALE

The basic rationale underlying this book is that active student involvement is necessary if education is to be meaningful. Rothkopf[6] has indicated that "in most instructional situations, what is learned depends largely on the activities of the student." Anderson[7] supports this thesis when he states that "the activities the student engages in when confronted with instructional tasks are of crucial importance in determining what he will learn."

Student involvement is crucial, and the asking of questions is central to this involvement, not just when something is not clear, but in actual dealing with information. The processing of information has a planning stage, a doing stage, and an evaluative or feedback stage. Learners must participate in all of these stages, and their engagement requires asking questions. Indeed, we might modify Rothkopf's statement and assert that in most instructional situations, what is learned depends largely on the activities *and the questions* of the student. The question is perhaps the primary tool by which the individual processes information regardless of the diversity of his procedures. Questions serve to focus student functioning and to provide a means for determining relevant from irrelevant information and for pointing up major relationships among information, as well as creating new insights and assessing the results of inquiry. Meaningful questions and questioning couched in student activities enable students also to gain understandings of their affective reactions to learning.

In recent years, increased attention has been given to the teacher's utilization of questions in the classroom. This is fine, but the major actor or actress in the learning drama should be the student. It is the student who should be engaged in the activities. Teachers have become more skilled questioners in many situations, and this is good, but they still must provide learners with opportunities to improve their questions and questioning skills.

MAKING STUDENT INVOLVEMENT
A REALITY

> What we know and how well we know it are the products
> of how we go about learning. The reverse is also true. How
> we go about learning is conditioned by what we know (and
> want to know) and how well we know it (and want to
> know it).[8]

This book intentionally takes a narrow focus on the questioning process, but it does not mean to imply that the activities discussed in later chapters are the sole ways to induce persons to learn or to excite them with the potentialities of the world of learning. Certainly, there are myriad techniques that one can incorporate and equal legions of procedures that learners can employ in their encounters with information. Variation does exist and this is good, but it does not negate the centrality of the question. But the reader should not interpret this centrality of the question to mean that the question has to be used in a narrow procedure, following precise steps carried out in a neat fashion. The argument for the use of questions does not imply that learning only can take place through an exact sequence of questions from the levels of knowledge through analysis, concluding with evaluation. This one way does suggest several related strategies, but there are numerous schema the teacher can utilize and these strategies draw upon different types of thinking. In addition to reflective thinking, we have critical thinking, creative thinking, and even such things as "intuitive leaps" in which persons accomplishing such "leaps" are hard put to explain how they arrived at their conclusions. Certainly, this book does not suggest that educators rule out possibilities for serendipity among ourselves or our pupils. We need to seek out the unexpected and to capitalize upon it when it occurs.

Beyer states that "the primary purpose of teaching is to facilitate learning—to stimulate it, guide it, direct it, make it easier, and in general ensure that it happens."[9] The activities

mentioned in this book hopefully will provide teachers with
some suggestions that will facilitate student learning, that will
stimulate, guide, and direct it; that will make it easier. The
encounters are offered as ways to increase the probability
that the questioner will learn.

   All of the activities suggest ways to involve the students.
Thier[10] discusses four levels of involvement in relation to
science, but the levels seem applicable to all subject areas.
The first level is minimal involvement: students reading about
something. The second level puts the learner in a higher
degree of involvement: becoming involved in classroom
discussions about some subject matter. Thier indicates that
this engagement is limited to verbal expressions. The third
level of involvement occurs when the teacher encourages the
learner to experiment or demonstrate using "Systems of
Objectives" of particular phenomena. The fourth and highest
stage of involvement is that at which the learner is totally
involved in observing and studying phenomena, recording
what occurs to them, and engaging in directly experiencing
the phenomena.

ORGANIZATION OF THE BOOK

The central portion of this text, chapters 4, 5, and 6, is not
designed in the standard manner. These chapters are
organized to focus on specific activities. Each activity is
presented with consideration of its rationale, description of
the particular activity with inclusion of sample sheets to use,
discussion of an example or examples using the activity, and
mention of any points that you should keep in mind when
considering the activity's use. The ideas in many of the
activity sheets can be used with many class members. It is
possible that older students may read these chapters of the
book themselves.

   Chapter 4 considers activities designed to involve students
in planning to use questions, while chapter 5 centers on

activities created to involve students in using their questions. Chapter 6 presents activities to engage students in assessing their questions and questioning procedures, as well as appraising the questions and procedures of others.

How to Use This Book

As indicated previously, this book is a response to the question frequently asked by teachers, "How do I get my students involved with working with questions, with understanding process?"

The teacher should consider this book a ready source when designing specific ways to involve students in processing information. Whatever type of thinking you expect to stimulate, mode of discovery you wish to stress, or model of teaching you intend to follow, these activities can be used in their basic form. Of course, the type of questions, the types of information, and the amount of structure provided by the teacher will vary according to which model of teaching is employed and which mode of discovery is emphasized (see chapter 7 for a discussion of models of teaching and modes of discovery).

When students are at the beginning of some class investigation, the teacher should refer to the book to determine ways to facilitate their planning and allow learners time to think carefully through their plans and questions. If students are engaged in some investigation, use of some of the involving activities will assist students by making their search more meaningful. Particular activities will often appeal to certain students because of their learning style.

When the students are concluding a lesson, the teacher should check to see what activities are appropriate in getting students to diagnose their processing of information, their asking of questions. These activities, despite their emphasis on students processing, planning to process, or assessing their processing, are not presented to construct a case for process over content. Indeed, there really can be no separation, for both are melded into the total experience of learning. No individual just learns process for the sake of process. A learner becoming knowledgeable about and skilled in process does so to grasp the world of knowledge more completely, to have a better hold on information so that it is more meaningful and more useful as she becomes or strives to become the independent learner.

The reader should not assume these activities to be exhaustive, but they will stimulate ideation of additional ones. As students become acquainted with these encounters, they also may think of diverse ways in which they can plan their questions or use them in particular manners.

This is a text that should be on the teacher's desk for formulating lesson plans. Hopefully, the reader will find it a valuable source for planning all aspects of instruction.

IMPLICATIONS

Involving students in their learning has implications for teacher roles, types of materials used, and the learning environment. The use of these activities and this approach to education also has implications for student roles as well.

The teacher needs to be a facilitator of learning and a manager of educational environments. Certainly teachers will present information at times, but their prime roles will be in the realm of providing learners with opportunities to become engaged in their own learning, not telling the learners what is important to know. Students do not have to discover the world again; not all learning advocated as beneficial is inductive. Indeed, not all inductive learning is open discovery (see chapter 7 for a discussion of open discovery) with few guidelines. Most of the students in school will be functioning within environments that have been structured— designed if you will—by teachers to encourage, guide, and sometimes assure that learners will engage in particular activities and arrive at specific understandings. But the important point is that the activities in this book require the teacher to take a facilitator role in the school. These activities are for the students!

There is no doubt that this type of teaching, allowing class "scholars" to engage in planning, to actually carry out their plans, and to assess the effectiveness of their strategies, is difficult from the standpoint of providing the necessary support for success, both psychological as well as material. Such student involvement takes time. Learning by experiencing process is not quick, and those teachers or those planning to be teachers will find it frustrating at times to watch as students, especially at the beginning stages, attempt to make meaningful plans and carry them out via particular uses of questions.

For these activities to be most productive, the teacher should arrange for numerous types of materials, verbal, visual, and auditory. Many of these activities will require that classes have access to much material. The teacher cannot plan investigations with only one text or posit meaningful questions if all the materials present are secondary sources.

Many of the activities we recommend can be conducted in the regular classroom, but others, especially in the doing or involvement stage, require the classroom to change from the standard format to perhaps one resembling a committee hearing room, a laboratory with demonstration tables, a press room for interviews, or a simulated environment in which various gaming can occur.

Quite often the activities involved in using questions in particular strategies require students to use their community as their learning environment. "School" is a place where individuals are involved in the processes of learning and therefore does not have to be limited to the "school building"; it can be any place where students can interact with others, with materials, with environmental variables. The educational environment can be any place where students can pose questions and obtain data.

All of this implies that the student has shifted from being rather passive—reading the book and answering the end-of-the-chapter questions—to being a person involved in making plans for learning, indicating what questions he or she will ask and outlining possible directions for future inquiries. The student role is one of a person totally involved in asking questions about data, about situations encountered in school situations, simulated situations, actual situations. The learner role is also that of a person involved in critiquing the questions he has raised, the procedures he has employed, and the sources he has checked, as well as the questions and procedures of others.

WAYS TO HELP STUDENTS BECOME INVOLVED

Students are not going to leap from being passive and highly dependent learners to independent processors of information in an instant. It will take time, and this time will vary depending upon the capabilities, interests, and backgrounds of the students. But it can, and it should happen to all students, not just the intellectually gifted.

Perhaps the best way for teachers to assist students to become involved is to indicate a genuine belief in the benefits accrued from involvement. The teacher has to believe in the process and believe that taking the time to plan questions and then carefully utilizing these questions has rewards that justify the energy expended. The teacher needs to be an exemplar of one who carefully plans questions and uses them to become more knowledgeable.

In addition, teachers should pose questions that will provide assistance for students. "What can I do to help you today?" should be asked. "How would you plan to get some information on this? Are there any other ways we can attack the problem? What do you suppose would happen if you used the questions in this sequence? What happened when you used this activity as opposed to the one we tried last week?" Questions like these will indicate to the student that the teacher does want to help. Then, as students use the activities suggested in this book, the teacher should arrange debriefing sessions to discuss the results obtained or the feelings present. It is most important for students to realize that the teacher is willing to listen to their affective responses.

The following questions can serve as a checklist for teachers to determine if they have been providing necessary help for students. Most of these questions relate to the activities presented in this book. The list is not exhaustive, but hopefully, it will encourage readers to generate other questions to determine if they are creating the classroom reality necessary for students to become really involved with their questions.

> Did I provide an atmosphere which was nonthreatening and which encouraged students to "blue sky" about the questions they wished to ask?
>
> Did I schedule opportunities for students to discuss their questions with fellow classmates, with me?
>
> Did I encourage student discussion of the consequences of the questions they asked?
>
> Did I offer specific suggestions to students about how to plan, recognize, and implement particular question types into certain strategies for processing information?
>
> Did I provide students with opportunities to test their questions in role playing or simulation?
>
> Did I, as the teacher, serve as an effective exemplar of the good questioner?
>
> Did I sit down with particular students or the class and discuss the dimensions of particular strategies and the place of the question in these strategies?
>
> Did I assign opportunities for students to analyze the questions of resource persons?

Did I discuss with students the task of analyzing questions they encountered in written materials?

Did I provide situations in which students planned games of recognizing certain types of questions and generating questions from materials encountered?

Did I give students time to try out their questions in mini-investigations to get "input" on the effectiveness of their questions?

Did I schedule opportunities for students to react cognitively and affectively to questions encountered or planned?

Did I give guidance to students in judging their questions on cognitive and affective levels?

Did I encourage and assist students in engaging in self-analysis relating to their questions?

Did I provide students with opportunities to learn about the criteria of effective questions and situations in which to apply these criteria to their own questions?

Did I schedule opportunities or allow students to schedule their own opportunities to analyze their questions and questioning techniques to determine if any problems existed?

WAYS TO CHECK STUDENT INVOLVEMENT

Not only must teachers develop means of assisting students to become involved with questions, but we must devise ways of assessing whether in fact learners are involved. Much of this information can be obtained from raising questions such as the following:

Who did most of the work in this class?

Who raised most of the questions?

Did I as teacher come across as the major performer?

Did the lesson reveal students doing things, or were they listening primarily to me?

In what activities were learners engaged?

Just what were learners doing?
How are classmates spending their free time?
What are they doing after class time?
Are they taking advantage of the interest centers?
Do I find many students conversing in teams about topics studied in class?

Answers to these questions should indicate to teachers the degree of student involvement and also whether students are being assisted in becoming more independent because of the teacher's action. The teacher can obtain information about whether or not the environment is conducive to student involvement. Do the data indicate adequate time allowed for projects, sufficient materials available, necessary psychological support present?

The Case Study

There are other more specific means for checking on student involvement. The teacher can do a case study on an individual or groups of individuals over a period of time relating to their involvement in class activities. The following case study is an example of a four-day observation of a student focusing on questions.

Case Study on Denise's Questions

DAY 1 OBSERVATION. From this first observation of Denise in social studies class discussion, it is evident that she only participates when she feels confident of the answer. Few questions are asked, and those are at the knowledge level.

DAY 2 OBSERVATION. Observed Denise today for ten minutes in social studies. She is responding to my encouragement to get involved in discussion. However, her questions, although more numerous, are still primarily at the knowledge level. She also is satisfied with one-word responses. She evidences some unsureness of her conclusions for she will question them if challenged by fellow classmates. I gave her some handouts on types of questions.

DAY 3 OBSERVATION: This observation relates to a class discussion six days after observation 2. I notice Denise is following my suggestion and jotted down a list of questions she wished to consider in the round table discussion today. The questions posed were at higher cognitive levels, comprehension and analysis. She also has begun to generate some questions relating to how she feels about the data and the situation encountered.

DAY 4 OBSERVATION. Today Denise raised a key question for consideration in social studies class. Her question was at the evaluation level and required the total class to consider on what basis they were going to judge the actions of the persons under consideration.

I am pleased with Denise's progress in generating higher-level questions and in planning questions before engaging in processing information. I feel that before long, I will no longer need to have briefing sessions with her in relation to her questioning.

Other Evaluative Systems

Formal systems, such as Flanders Interaction Analysis Categories, are available for teachers' use. This analysis provides some information relating to questions as well as to the degree of authoritarian and nonauthoritarian traits of the teacher. There is a legion of instruments for the analysis of classroom dialogue. Regarding the specific analysis of student involvement with questions, the Teacher-Pupil Question Inventory developed by Davis and Tinsely[11] provides specific information about the number and types of questions learners are asking and responding to as well as similar information regarding teacher's questions.

Determining the degree of student participation in questioning can be accomplished using some of the standard diagnostic or evaluation means: anecdotal records, sociograms, individual progress reports, and checklists. Much of the assessment of student activity can be handled by the learners themselves.

WHAT SHOULD WE BE TEACHING OUR STUDENTS?

Individuals are characterized by what they know, but more importantly, by what they do—their behavior. Those who discuss values and valuing indicate that someone really does not have a value until he organizes it, internalizes it, and utilizes it so that he is characterized by it. Teachers should provide each student with experiences that will enable him not only to be knowledgeable of the question and its place in process, but to value the question and process to the degree that he utilizes questions in such ways that others recognize in him a person excited by questions, by the world of learning, and an individual determined to make his contribution to himself and his world. As we influence the students in the classroom regarding the use of the question, the use of process, so will they perceive process in their lives.

Involving students with questions within the context of process certainly is not educational salvation, but it most assuredly provides a step in the right direction for furnishing students with opportunities to deal with their ever-expanding, ever-changing world.

Yamamoto mentions that "Indeed, each tree is known by its own fruit. . ."[12] and we cannot expect to gather figs from thorns or grapes from a bramble bush. If we place a premium on the passive and reactive mind, that is precisely what we get.[13]

The paramount tasks set for us are those relating to the cultivation of competence and the search for human identity.[14] The involvement of students in these various stages of activity should contribute to the competence dimension and even the search for human identity. Hopefully, if we schedule the time for the development of competence in process, students will realize the challenge and become committed to understanding people and their world, all dimensions of their world.

We should be teaching our students means by which they can reach their potential and achieve an excitement for learning, for being involved with the myriad realms of knowledge. Perhaps one might state that we should be teaching our students the need for total involvement, not just in the short-range view of performance in school but in the long-range view of the rest of their lives.

Whether we as educators or potential educators are successful depends in part upon how well we believe in these tasks ourselves and how willing we are to make the extra effort to assure that students have the time, materials, skills, environments, and encouragement necessary for total involvement in process. Our success also depends upon whether we have organized the learning experiences of students in such ways that the students are willing also to make the extra effort for total involvement. If, in the long range, students do not reach full competence or contribute to the best degree, then we share part of their failure. If our students are successful, we share partly in their success.

CONCLUDING NOTES

This chapter presented the reader with the purpose of the book: to provide in-service teachers and prospective teachers with activities that will enable students to be involved in planning their use of questions, actually carrying out their plans, and assessing the effectiveness of their procedures utilizing questions. The main rationale of the book is to stress the crucial nature of student involvement and the place of questions in that involvement.

Discussion centered on how to make student involvement a reality as well as specific suggestions for the use of this textbook. Comments on organization of the book indicated that the main portion will deal with student activities for planning, doing, and assessing questions. The format of the activities was presented: basic rationale, activity description, example, and other pertinent information.

We stressed that this was not a book to be read from beginning to end, but rather one to be used continually when planning ways to involve students in their learning.

Implications were indicated for readers following the suggestions in the book. New roles for both teacher and student were implied, with the teacher becoming more of a facilitator of learning and the student becoming more the prime performer. Ways to check student involvement were considered, with the reader considering a specific case study.

The chapter concluded with a treatment of what we should be teaching our students. These last pages indicated that the type of student we get is the type of student we foster in the classroom. Yamamoto maintained that we have, by our actions, stressed the development of a student with a passive and reactive mind. If we wish to encourage active students, then we need to let them assume a major role in question asking.

NOTES

1. CHARLES DeGARMO, *Interest and Education. The Doctrine of Interest and Its Concrete Application* (New York: The Macmillan Co., 1911), p. 226.

2. FRANCIS P. HUNKINS, *Questioning Strategies and Techniques* (Boston: Allyn and Bacon, Inc., 1972).

3. CARL R. ROGERS, *Client Centered Therapy* (Boston: Houghton Mifflin, 1951), p. 427.

4. ARTHUR A. CARIN and ROBERT B. SUND, *Developing Questioning Techniques, A Self-Concept Approach* (Columbus, Ohio: Charles E. Merrill Publishing Co., 1971), p. 39.

5. Ibid., p. 44.

6. ERNST ROTHKOPF, "The Concept of Mathemagenic Activities," *Review of Educational Research* 40 (1970): 325-336.

7. RICHARD C. ANDERSON, "Control of Students Mediating Process During Verbal Learning and Instruction," *Review of Educational Research* 40 (1970): 349-369.

8. BARRY K. BEYER, *Inquiry in the Social Studies Classroom: A Strategy for Teaching* (Columbus, Ohio: Charles E. Merrill Publishing Co., 1971), p. 9.

9. Ibid., p. 9.

10. HERBERT D. THIER, "The Involvement of Children in the Science Program," *Science and Children* Vol. II (February 1965).

11. O. L. DAVIS, JR. and DREW C. TINSLEY, "Cognitive Objectives Revealed by Classroom Questions Asked by Social Studies Student Teachers," *Peabody Journal of Education* 45, No. 1 (July 1967).

12. KAORU YAMAMOTO, *Teaching* (Boston: Houghton Mifflin Co., 1969), p. 225.

13. Ibid.

14. Ibid., p. 256.

2

Questions in the Cognitive Domain

For the educator to assist students in becoming skilled questioners, he or she must be knowledgeable about the types of questions that can be generated in the cognitive domain. This chapter provides an overview of Bloom's taxonomy of educational objectives in the cognitive domain, and examples of questions at these levels. Key words to assist the teacher to recognize questions at specific cognitive levels also are presented. The chapter also presents information to enable teachers to work with questions at various cognitive levels.

BLOOM'S TAXONOMY OF EDUCATIONAL OBJECTIVES: COGNITIVE DOMAIN[1]

Knowledge

KNOWLEDGE. Knowledge involves the recall of specifics and universals, the recall of methods and processes, or the recall of a pattern, structure, or setting.

Knowledge of Specifics. Knowledge of specifics involves the recall of specific and isolable bits of information, knowledge of terminology, and knowledge of specific facts.

Knowledge of Ways and Means of Dealing with Specifics. This subdivision has the following categories:

> Knowledge of conventions
> Knowledge of trends and sequences
> Knowledge of classifications and categories
> Knowledge of criteria
> Knowledge of methodology.

Knowledge of the Universals and Abstractions in a Field. This subdivision has the following categories:

> Knowledge of principles and generalizations
> Knowledge of theories and structures.

Intellectual Abilities and Skills

COMPREHENSION. This cognitive level refers to a type of understanding or apprehension which implies that the individual knows what is being communicated and can make use of the material or idea being communicated without necessarily relating it to other material or seeing its fullest implications.

Translation. Comprehension as evidenced by the care and accuracy with which the communication is paraphrased or rendered from one language or communication to another.

Interpretation. The explanation or summarization of a communication.

Extrapolation. The extension of trends or tendencies beyond the given data to determine implications, consequences, corollaries, effects, etc., which are in accordance with the conditions described in the original communication.

APPLICATION. This is the use of abstractions in particular and concrete situations. The abstractions may be in the form of general ideas, rules of procedure, or generalized methods.

ANALYSIS. Analysis is the breakdown of a communication into its constituent elements or parts.

Analysis of Elements. Identification of the elements included in a communication.

Analysis of Relationships. The connections and interactions between elements and parts of a communication.

Analysis of Organizational Principles. The organization, systematic arrangement, and structure which hold the communication together.

SYNTHESIS. Synthesis is the putting together of elements and parts to form a whole.

Production of a Unique Communication. The development of a communication in which the writer or speaker attempts to convey ideas, feelings, and/or experiences to others.

Production of a Plan, or Proposed Set of Operations. The development of a plan or the proposal of a plan of operations.

Derivation of a Set of Abstraction Relations. The development of a set of abstract relations either to classify or explain particular data or phenomena; or the deduction of propositions and relations from a set of basic propositions or symbolic representations.

EVALUATION. Evaluation calls for making judgments about the value of material and methods for given purposes.

Judgments in Terms of Internal Evidence. Evaluation of the accuracy of a communication from such evidence as logical accuracy, consistency, and other internal criteria.

Judgments in Terms of External Criteria. Evaluation of material with reference to selected or remembered criteria.

QUESTIONS AT VARIOUS COGNITIVE LEVELS

KNOWLEDGE QUESTIONS

According to Bloom's classification scheme, the first type of question is the knowledge question, and several subtypes exist. Knowledge of specifics is the first general heading and questions under this heading focus on knowledge of terminology. Consider the examples that follow.

Examples

What is the meaning of inflation?
What is a synapse?
What is free verse?
What is an isotope?
What is meant by alpha level in statistics?

These questions just inquire whether learners understand specific terms, not whether they can process information.

The second subcategory under knowledge of specifics is *knowledge of specific facts.* Such questions center on facts with no attempt made to ascertain if learners know the value of the facts or truly understand the particular facts recalled.

Consider the following examples. Ask yourself how these questions differ from the previous examples. Are there any key words at the beginning of these questions that will give you a clue to their cognitive level? How do these questions compare with the ones you utilize in your class or have incorporated into lesson plans? What other questions can you generate at this cognitive level? Do you feel that these questions are worthwhile?

Examples

What state grows the most lettuce?

When is Columbus Day?

When does school get out?

The Monroe Doctrine was created
   a. to encourage the development of the New World.
   b. to prevent foreign powers from obtaining a control in the New World.
   c. to assure that the U.S. Navy would remain strong.
   d. to prevent the outbreak of war.

Today the percentage of persons living in urban areas is
   a. about 50 percent.
   b. about 90 percent.
   c. about 70 percent.
   d. about 40 percent.

In plane geometry, the shortest distance between two points is
   a. a straight line.
   b. a curved line.
   c. an elliptical line.
   d. dependent upon line conditions.

Indicate what is meant by surrealistic art.
   a. art dealing with abstract forms.
   b. art dealing with subdued colors.
   c. art dealing with realistic presentations in unnatural and unusual ways.
   d. art dealing with the use of numerous fine points of color blended for a hazy effect.

TEACHER ACTIVITIES

While reacting to these examples, the reader is encouraged to generate additional ones. Record your responses to the questions. Note that the examples, although requiring knowledge, really do not demand students to work with information. All they have to do is recall information previously read or discussed in class.

The second major division under knowledge is *knowledge of ways and means of dealing with specific facts.* The first subdivision of this category is *knowledge of conventions.* Analyze the following examples.

Examples

How many players do we need for a football team?

How do you spell Mississippi?

What is the proper use of the salad fork?

Underline the proper word in the space provided:

My brother and (me, I) went to the fair.

My father gave (me, I) a book for Christmas.

Indicate how the following words would change if spoken with a Boston accent, Brooklyn accent, Midwest (Illinois) accent, West Coast accent (California).

idea,   father,   often,   India,   aunt

These questions require cognizance of the ways one can react to and deal with information and reality, but they do not require learners to initiate any action. Students are functioning strictly on the verbal recall level.

Note that these questions begin with various words, not just with "what." The first two questions start with how, which often is interpreted to mean questions aimed at higher levels of thinking. But the wording of questions can be misleading; it is the overall intent of the question that suggests its cognitive level.

Questions at the next sublevel of knowledge, *knowledge of trends and sequences,* ask individuals to express awareness of happenings and to indicate when they occurred according to a time reference. However, students are not required to do anything beyond this. As you consider the ensuing examples you may think of content areas in which such questions might be phrased.

Examples

What steps does one follow in directing a bill through Congress?

What is the procedure for working through a continuous progress school?

List the major steps in making a cake.

Indicate four major happenings that have affected our society at large during the last three years.

Which are the correct stages in the life of a silkworm?

  a. adult, egg, larva.
  b. egg, adult, larva.
  c. egg, larva, adult.
  d. adult, larva, egg.

TEACHER ACTIVITIES

Again, record your reactions to these questions.
Develop your own questions at this cognitive level.
How do they compare with the examples?

Often, in classes stressing process, students are asked to observe various phenomena and to classify them according to some criteria. In order to function at this higher level, learners must first be cognizant of particular classifications. Questions for this sublevel of knowledge, *knowledge of classifications and categories,* follow.

Examples

To what classification does the silk moth belong?

An orthopedist is a person who
  a. works with bone ailments.
  b. specializes in the treatment of feet.
  c. specializes in the treatment of children.
  d. works in the area of general medicine.

The discipline which deals with people and their relationship to earth is
  a. history.
  b. sociology.
  c. geography.
  d. economics.
  e. anthropology.

Indicate the major schools of European art.

The number 4 is a
  a. cardinal number.
  b. ordinal number.
  c. fractional number.
  d. real number.

A boy sees a picture advertising food and his mouth waters. This type of response is an example of
  a. chaining.
  b. stimulus response.
  c. signal learning.
  d. verbal and visual association.
  e. concept learning.

These questions are becoming more difficult in some instances, but they are still not asking for the student to function at any higher cognitive level. He still only needs to "know" what the classifications and categories are. He does not have to invent classifications, nor does he have to categorize new data with which he is unfamiliar.

TEACHER ACTIVITIES

Record your reactions to these questions. Make a list of questions you think are also at this level. How do your questions compare? How do you like them? Do you think your questions will trigger not only response by your students but also interest in the content area concerned?

When information is discussed or conclusions are advanced, learners must judge such end products by their appropriateness, but judgments cannot be made in ignorance of criteria. There are questions that both teacher and students can pose that aim at assessing whether one has *knowledge of criteria*. Consider these examples.

Examples

How can we tell when we are being effective students?

What are three criteria by which we can assess the quality of a television program?

According to research principles, a good experiment is

    a. one which duplicates the practical world.

    b. one which randomizes groups and controls the significant variables.

    c. one which selects groups from the nearest population at hand.

    d. one which extends the experiment over the greatest period of time.

A good principle in pest control is

    a. to hit the population when it begins to increase in numbers.

    b. to utilize compounds of high toxicity.

    c. to attack the population when it begins recovery with compounds with a long life of toxicity.

    d. to repeatedly apply the chemical.

Note that the students only have to reiterate criteria heard or read. Even though some of the questions might be judged as quite difficult, there is no demand made on the students to apply the criteria recognized or recalled in any sort of way. Also, reflect on the format of the questions; some are complete sentence, others are multiple choice. Format does not directly influence cognitive or affective level. One can have multiple choice questions at all major levels, but there are some sublevels of the taxonomy at which one has to rely more heavily or exclusively on one particular format. For example, questions at the first two sublevels of synthesis, to be discussed later, should be posed in essay format, for one cannot write an objective question having a multiple choice format requiring a student to create a unique response.

TEACHER ACTIVITIES

Attend to the examples of the questions designed to test knowledge of criteria. Ask yourself about your reactions to these questions. What questions can you write at this level? In what areas of content would you feel comfortable writing questions at this cognitive level? Perhaps you can record your reactions on a data chart along with your reactions to the previous examples.

Educators are presently very concerned with involving students in methods of investigation or discovery. However, before learners can utilize various methods they must understand them and realize their basic steps. Educators and educators-to-be need to formulate questions that query individuals regarding their *knowledge of methodology.* Analyze the following examples.

Examples

What is one way we can study the intestines of the frog?
What are the basic steps in organizing a term paper?
What procedures can one follow in preparing for a debate?

The Periodic Table can be used to
a. determine the atomic weights of compounds.
b. estimate the effectiveness of a chemical reaction.
c. assist in the discovery of new elements.
d. determine the compatibility of various elements.

The procedure for making an oil painting usually requires that the artist first
a. select colors.
b. sketch the basic composition.
c. begin painting the background in oils.
d. begin applying paint in a random fashion.

List the major steps you would follow in solving a problem in your general mathematics class.

Again, these questions do not require that students actually apply some methodology to a particular task or situation; rather, they demand only an indication that the student has cognizance of the methodology in question.

TEACHER ACTIVITIES

Record your reactions to these questions. Try your hand at writing questions at this cognitive level. How do you react to your questions?

The last major division under the knowledge category is *knowledge of universals and abstractions in a field.* This classification is subdivided into *knowledge of principles and generalizations* and *knowledge of theories and structures.* Questions at these subdivisions do not require learners to discover or apply such information to any situation in or outside of the classroom. These questions focus on whether students know and can recall verbally or in writing principles, generalizations, theories, and structures. Of course, one might find that a student could verbalize a principle but upon further questioning really not know what it meant or how to apply it. This is one reason that educators need to phrase questions at various cognitive levels to give students opportunities and challenges to really demonstrate whether or not they can utilize particular aspects of knowledge.

Examples

$E=Mc^2$ refers to
    a. Darwin's theory of evolution.
    b. a theory to explain environmental balance.
    c. Einstein's theory of relativity.
    d. Oppenheimer's theory of atomic power.

The basic structure of geography centers around the concept of
    a. man.
    b. region.
    c. globe.
    d. time.

The concept of interdependence is crucial for understanding nations in today's world. Which of the following generalizations relate to the concept of interdependence?
    a. The affairs of human societies have historical antecedents and consequences.
    b. No nation or state is an island unto itself.
    c. Areas of the earth develop bonds, interconnections, and relations with other areas.
    d. Economic resources can be used in many ways.

These questions can be considered difficult, but remember that difficulty level is independent of cognitive level. In writing questions, you must be mindful of both factors.

TEACHER ACTIVITIES

Record your reactions to the questions. Write some

questions at this level. How do your questions compare? What are the major characteristics of your questions at these levels?

The previous exemplars at the various cognitive levels are not presented as the last word on question types, but are offered in hopes of enabling you to begin to nurture a more complete understanding of and a positive affect for questions at these several levels of knowledge.

Knowledge Questions—Key Words

Learners just beginning to develop questions at specific cognitive and affective levels want clues by which they can recognize types of questions as well as hints for construction of such questions. There are some fairly good indicators, but the reader must bear in mind that the level of a question is not only determined by its wording but also by the context in which it is phrased and the prior information a student brings to the situation in which the question is generated.

The following key words can be used as indicators of questions at the knowledge level.[2]

What	Distinguish	Recall	Write
When	Identify	Reorganize	Which
Who	List	Show	Indicate
Define	Name	State	Tell
Describe			How

COMPREHENSION QUESTIONS

Comprehension has three subdivisions, the first of which is *translation*. Questions at this level ask students to translate or paraphrase a communication from one form to another.

Examples

Draw a picture of what you did last summer.

What does he mean when he says "My kingdom for a
   horse?"

Explain in your own words the meaning of the diagram.[3]

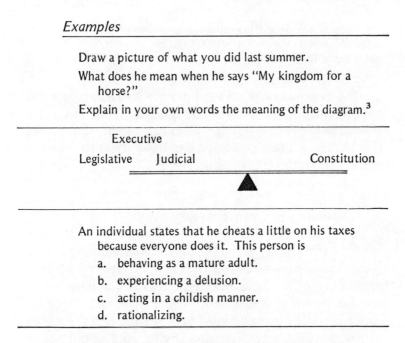

An individual states that he cheats a little on his taxes
   because everyone does it. This person is
   a. behaving as a mature adult.
   b. experiencing a delusion.
   c. acting in a childish manner.
   d. rationalizing.

The first question is quite common in the lower grades
when a teacher asks children to draw a picture of a story they
have just read or tell a story from an observation of a
picture. The question dealing with the diagram would not be
uncommon at the upper elementary level. The multiple
choice example could be phrased at any level of schooling.

Questions at the translation level emphasize putting some
communication into another language, into other terms, or
reproducing the communication in another form of communication. The individual dealing with these questions
must know what the question implies, but he or she also
must be cognizant of ways to put particular information into
another form. Specifically, the student is asked to commence putting knowledge to work.

TEACHER ACTIVITIES

React to the questions. Write some questions of your
own at this level and compare yours to the examples

provided. How do you react to your questions cognitively? Affectively? Record your reactions on a data chart.

The second level of comprehension is *interpretation,* and questions at this level require the student to derive the essential meaning of a communication from the question. The person is directed to the interrelationships found in the materials presented. Basically, these types of questions are after the central meaning of material being read or situations being encountered. However, these questions do not require the student to discern difficult implications.

React to the following examples.

Examples

> According to the story we read, which option indicates the author's main point about schools in America?
>
> What does the chart tell us?
>
> Compare the educational ideas of Dewey, Bruner, and Conant with regard to the involvement of students in their learning.
>
> Compare the reasons why the United States and Canada developed a system of superhighways.
>
> Discuss some of the differences between the American way of life and the Canadian way of life.
>
> Indicate those situations in which one would use the mean, the mode, and the median in discussing students' learning in the area of mathematics.

TEACHER ACTIVITIES

We ask many questions at this level in our classrooms to ascertain if students grasp what they are reading. What did the author say? What are the main points? How well do you understand the material you have encountered?

List some of your reactions to the examples. Record your cognitive and affective responses. Write some samples of your own.

The last level of comprehension is *extrapolation,* and
questions at this level urge students to go beyond a recount-
ing of the basic idea of material read or situation encountered. These questions challenge learners to formulate
an inference or inferences. With the current stress on being
prepared for the future, teacher and student questions at this
level should be evident in school dialogue. The examples
presented quite likely would appear in many classrooms.

Examples

From studying the corrections on your paper, what would
you conclude?

What do you think space travel will be like in the next
century?

Today, we are reading about projections relating to various
aspects of life in the future. What are some cautions we
need to apply to our reading of these projections?

Study the chemical composition of wood and write a list of
possible future uses of wood other than for building.

These questions request students to read between the
lines. Practice in extrapolation is crucial in today's world;
therefore, students need to experience these questions in
class discussions. More importantly, they need opportunities
to formulate such questions themselves as they process information.

Comprehension Questions—
Key Words

Teachers are greatly assisted in formulating or recognizing questions at particular levels if they have a list of key
words to help in identifying specific types of questions. The

following key words should provide help in recognizing and formulating comprehension questions.[4]

Compare	Distinguish	What
Conclude	Estimate	Fill in
Contrast	Explain	Give an example of
Demonstrate	Extend	Hypothesize
Differentiate	Extrapolate	Illustrate
Predict	Rearrange	Infer
Reorder	Rephrase	Relate
		Tell in your own words
Which		Inform

APPLICATION QUESTIONS

Application questions are concerned with engaging students in applying successfully some understanding or technique to a problem situation. Sometimes these questions only ask for the application of a principle without demanding a complete processing of the data or situation. Mathematics and science are two areas where one would expect to hear these questions, but hopefully, these questions would be present in dialogue relating to all curricular areas. The emphasis on process and means of discovery certainly requires such questions.

Examples

If Tom Sawyer can paint a fence alone in three days, how long will it take him if he has three friends do it for him, assuming each friend can work at the same speed as Tom?

Consider the map showing the topographic features of a region as well as roadways and population distribution. Assume you are an urban planner. Indicate where you

would locate a shopping center and explain the reasons
for the site you choose.

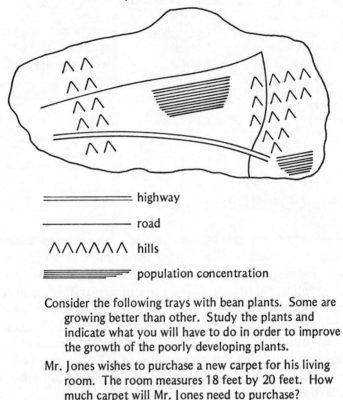

======================= highway

————————————————— road

∧∧∧∧∧∧ hills

≡≡≡≡≡≡≡ population concentration

Consider the following trays with bean plants. Some are
growing better than other. Study the plants and
indicate what you will have to do in order to improve
the growth of the poorly developing plants.

Mr. Jones wishes to purchase a new carpet for his living
room. The room measures 18 feet by 20 feet. How
much carpet will Mr. Jones need to purchase?

These questions require students to identify the problem
and then to recognize some principle or procedure for solution. These examples demand that students solve the
problem. However, in some instances, students only would
have to identify the correct procedure and not actually
engage in solution.

TEACHER ACTIVITIES

Develop some application questions of your own.
Compare your questions to the samples. What do you

think of yours? Record your reactions on a data chart.

Application Questions—
Key Words

Key words useful for guiding education students, teachers, and classroom students in formulating application questions follow:[5]

Apply	Build	Construct	Demonstrate
Develop	Plan	Solve	Indicate
Test	Choose	Show your work	Check out
Consider	How would	Tell us	

ANALYSIS QUESTIONS

Questions at the first level of analysis, *analysis of elements*, require students to diagnose materials, situations, or environments and to separate them into their component parts. With the emphasis in schools upon concept formation as well as more sophisticated understanding of primary and secondary sources, these questions should comprise much classroom dialogue. Some examples are presented below.

Examples

From our discussion on human behavior, what are two basic assumptions we must accept regarding people?

Putting all plants in the sun will make them grow to their maximum height. Is this a fact or an hypothesis? Analyze your materials and experimental results.

Job hiring agencies need to make every effort to consider minorities among the applications. When two people

are equally qualified for the job, the individual representing the minority should be give the first consideration. This directive, which is a part of Affirmative
Action, is based on the assumption
a. that minorities are more effective workers.
b. that minorities have been discriminated against in
   the past.
c. that minorities have a greater need for employment.
d. that people need to experience the views of
   minorities in their everyday experience.
Arguments for national health insurance are based primarily
on the belief that
a. such insurance would provide health care treatment.
b. present health care treatment is too expensive.
c. private health care leaves gaps in the coverage.
d. all of the above.

Questions at this level of analysis stress that students
react to unstated assumptions, distinguish facts from
hypotheses, discriminate among the various types of behavior
and motives of individuals, and identify a conclusion from
statements which support it. The student is actively engaged
with data, for these questions demand that he process information. Memory or comprehension is a necessary, but not a
sufficient condition for successful functioning with these
questions.

TEACHER ACTIVITIES

Record your own reactions to these questions and
write some questions of your own.

The second level of analysis is *analysis of relationships,*
and such questions direct learners' attention to relationships
between and among various elements recognized in the first
stage of analysis. If a teacher had asked students to identify
specific concepts or elements, in a previous lesson, she might
employ questions at this second level to have students discern
the relationships present between and among some of the
concepts.

Examples

Do the data support the hypothesis that women are not treated equally?

Support your conclusion from the information you have processed.

A group of college students were discussing the relative merits of two grading systems. It had been suggested that only two grades be used: S (satisfactory) and U (unsatisfactory), instead of the A-B-C-D-F system then in use at the college. One student made the following statement:

"People go to college to learn, not just to get grades. Grades are no indication of absolute degree of learning, they are purely relative and then mostly determined by chance or probability (guessing, multiple-choice tests, etc.). The student is a better judge of how he is doing than the professor. Therefore an S-U system would be better since it would cut down the amount of differentiation between grades and give a better picture of how the student is doing."

The conclusion depends fundamentally on the proposition that

a. people do not go to college just to get grades.
b. the student is the best judge of how he or she is doing.
c. grades are very inaccurate indications of what students have learned.
d. one grading system is better than the other.
e. multiple-choice tests are used in determining grades.

Which of the following statements is *least* essential as a part of the argument?

a. Grades are no indication of absolute degree of learning.
b. An S-U system would cut down the amount of differentiation between grades.
c. An S-U system would give a better picture of how the student is doing.
d. Grades are determined by chance or probability.
e. The student is a better judge of how he or she is doing than the professor.[6]

Questions at this level of analysis aim at engaging students in formal, though logical, reasoning. However, the logic does not have to be so precise as to eliminate students in the lower grades from using it. Children in elementary school do think and are logical to a degree appropriate for their age and maturity. They can deal with assumptions and hypotheses and can determine if sufficient data are present to support accepting an hypothesis. Of course, in writing questions at this cognitive level the teacher should exercise caution as to the difficulty level of the questions. Easy analysis questions might be appropriate for the lower grades, questions with easy meaning whose underlying assumptions are quite evident with a little reading.

TEACHER ACTIVITIES

Try writing some questions at this level. At first, it may seem a little difficult, but as you consider the components and characteristics of this type of question, the writing will become easier.

Questions representing the final category of analysis, *analysis of organization principles,* are posed to get students to grasp a communication or situation as a whole. The thrust of such questions is to direct students to understand how a certain material or situation "hangs" together as a whole, the Gestalt of the situation. How do all the concepts and their interrelationships relate to the total situation? These types of questions should be part of educational dialogue with students creating their own questions.

Examples

> What do you think was the artist's reason for painting this picture?
>
> From observation of the play *Hair,* what do you think was the playwright's major theme?

"Some people are more equal than others." Describe the
process by which the individual who voiced this phrase
arrived at his conclusion.

In Leonard Bernstein's Symphony "The Mass" the theme is
carried essentially by

a. the woodwinds.

b. the strings.

c. the brasses.

d. the percussion.

e. all of the above.

TEACHER ACTIVITIES

Write some questions at this level in your notebook.
Compare your questions with the examples. What are
the major features of your questions, the examples?
Is the cognitive intent clear?

Analysis Questions—
Key Words

Teachers and students often have difficulty distinguishing between analysis and comprehension questions, for
the initial words of both question types can be the same.
Perhaps it will help to think of comprehension questions as
aksing for "common sense" analysis while analysis questions
are more concerned with the rules of logic or the syntactical
rules of a particular discipline. Much depends upon the
context in which the question is asked as well as the information that the student brings to the situation in ascertaining
whether a question is indeed at the analysis level.

Analyze	Discriminate	Relate
Categorize	Distinguish	Explain
Describe	Recognize	What assumption
Classify	Support your	What do you[7]
Compare	Indicate the	

SYNTHESIS QUESTIONS

The cognitive level of synthesis also has three sublevels, the
first of which is asking individuals to produce something
unique to them, *production of a unique communication.* To
assess such questions the teacher doesn't have to judge the
product produced, but only query whether the questions do
indeed require the learners to organize their information to
produce a product unique to them. Consider the examples
provided below:

Examples

Write a poem to express your feelings about freedom.

Write a five-minute speech on the benefits of brushing after
every meal.

Write a defense of the need for wise use of our resources.

Write a paper on U.S. population distribution in the next
two decades.

Note that these questions wouldn't take too long to ask,
but time is required for the student to respond to them. The
second and third examples might easily be utilized in the
lower grades. The last example might be used at the upper
grades, but could be used at lower grades as well. What
would change would be the degree of sophistication of
response expected by you at the particular level of your class.

TEACHER ACTIVITIES

Note your reactions to these questions and write
some examples of your own. Would you classify your
questions as easy or difficult? Why would you ask the
questions you have formulated? Do they really
benefit the student?

Production of a plan is the second level of synthesis, and
this type of question requests the student to produce a plan

or generate a solution satisfactory to the requirements of a particular task. Again, the teacher has to wait until the plan is produced or solution carried out to see if the learner has responded adequately to the question, but this in no way detracts from the question. It is not uncommon for good questions to elicit less than quality responses at this level; responses depend primarily upon the learner's ability, interest in the topic, the stress given to the topic in class, and the time available for dealing with the question. The teacher should assist the learner to respond to the most optimal degree possible.

Examples

Indicate a way in which learners can progress through the school sequence more quickly.

How can we get the community to support special school levies?

Many people are spending more time outdoors. Design a recreation deck for the home in our diagram that will consider the traffic flow in the house and the contour and space present in the yard.

Devise a plan by which you can get the community to be conservation conscious.

Create a proof for the following equation using what information you know about the binary system of numbers.

TEACHER ACTIVITIES

Try creating some examples of your own. Do your questions get students involved in actually doing something, either verbally or physically? Are students forced to create something that is their own, or are they just regurgitating a plan that they read of some previous time?

The final level of synthesis is *derivation of a set of abstract relations,* and questions here invite students to create or derive some type of statement or conclusion to explain or

classify information from data or situations they can
analyze. Such questions are concerned primarily with
students' ability to formulate generalizations. With the
emphasis upon both inductive and deductive discovery, these
questions should be common in both teachers' and students'
repertoires.

Examples
_____

From our experiments with plants and different types of
    soil, what statement can we formulate regarding plant
    growth?
Drawing on your experiences in school, how do people view
    education in this country?
What major hypothesis can you generate addressed to the
    high standard of living in the United States?
From the writings on educational theory, what would be
    the two major ways in which theory can be considered?
_____

TEACHER ACTIVITIES

Record your reactions to these questions. How do
these questions differ from the previous synthesis
examples? Which questions did you find easiest to
create? Which questions do you think your students
or students-to-be would find easiest to process?
Record your reactions on a data chart.

*Synthesis Questions—
Key Words*

Write	Suggest	Plan
Think of a way	How	Formulate a solution
Create	Develop	
Propose a plan	Make up	Synthesize
Put together	What conclusion	Derive[8]

What would be
What major hypothesis

EVALUATION QUESTIONS

Questions at the first stage of evaluation, *judgments in terms
of internal evidence,* request students to analyze data or conclusions from standpoints such as logical accuracy, consistency, and other internal criteria. Students responding to or
creating their own questions at this level are dealing with the
tasks of judging, appraising, or valuing. Some examples for
consideration follow.

Examples

Which statement below would explain whether the painting
  is one of high quality?

Has Charlie made a good case for reducing the time required for learning elementary physics?

Mr. Jones presented his case last night for increased trade
  with Communist China. He indicated that if we trade
  with China, their economy will become dependent in
  part upon our economy, and this being the case, the
  tendency for belligerent conflict will be reduced.
  Analyze Mr. Jones' argument and indicate whether his
  thinking is on sound or shaky ground.

The use of dance for interpretation should not be part of
  the schools, for dancing is primarily a medium of expression for women in our culture and it should so
  remain. If we force men into a dance in school situations, we do not create appreciation, but rather destroy
  the masculine role as defined by the larger society.

Explain any fallacies in reasoning which may exist in the
  above statement.

These examples require active student involvement.
Students are required to select the appropriate criteria upon

which to make evaluative judgments. The teacher does not
inform the students what these criteria are. If he did, the
students would really only be applying known criteria to a
particular situation, and not really functioning at the
valuative level.

TEACHER ACTIVITIES

Create some questions of your own. How do you like
yours? Evaluate your questions using some of the
criteria that have been implied and mentioned regarding the creation of effective questions at the specific
cognitive levels.

The second sublevel of evaluation, *judgments in terms of
external criteria,* deals with the evaluation in terms of external criteria and such questions require the student to apply
known criteria to judge situations, conclusions or objectives
that he or she has encountered or developed. This is a most
crucial stage of questioning for it directs learners to consider
if their conclusions, their findings, are warranted and worth
keeping.

Examples

Indicate in what ways this is a beautiful poem.

According to the stated situation, which is the most
appropriate move the man could take?

Analyze the transportation network in your community
and list all of the aspects you consider to be positive
factors and explain your reasons for the choices.

Judge the list of questions that you have created and
indicate why you consider them to be effective and at
specific cognitive levels.

The examples indicate questions to which the student
would respond by engaging in evaluative functioning utilizing
criteria formulated by experts in the field. Being cognizant
of these criteria, the student recognizes that here is a situa-

tion or situations in which he or she needs to apply these criteria in order to make a required judgment. It is the student who recognizes the need for certain criteria and also who makes the selection as to which criteria are precisely appropriate. Sometimes we ask questions resembling these but provide so many clues relating to criteria that students are really only applying known criteria to the situation rather than determining for themselves which criteria are indeed necessary. This may be fine at certain times in the classroom, but not at those instances in which we wish students to be engaged in evaluative functioning.

Evaluation Questions— Key Words

With evaluation questions the teacher often needs to consider phrases rather than single words as indicators. Questions beginning with *what, which,* and *who* can be evaluative in how they ask students to make selections about *what* is most appropriate, *which* person is most effective, and *who* did the most appropriate thing in this situation.

What is	Select
Choose	Which would you consider
Evaluate	Defend
Decide	Check
Judge	What is most appropriate[9]
Check the	
Indicate	

WORKING WITH QUESTIONS IN THE COGNITIVE DOMAIN

Look at Question Types

It is one thing to read about questions at several cognitive levels and to study examples; it is quite another thing to create questions at these cognitive levels. In order to get a handle on questions at various cognitive levels the reader must engage in some examination of the sample questions. What are the major features of questions at each cognitive level or sublevel? With what words do questions at the knowledge level start? Identify the student action implied in the questions' wording. Explain the differences of questions at various cognitive sublevels.

Record the differences in the wording of the questions at various cognitive levels. How do the questions at one cognitive level differ from questions at another cognitive level? Identify the intent you derive from carefully comparing a comprehension question with a knowledge question. Describe how format changes the cognitive level of questions. Infer the situation in which certain questions might be asked.

If you have been writing some examples of questions at each of the cognitive levels as you read this chapter, go back and reconsider them now. Compare then again to the examples. Ask some of the questions indicated above about your questions. Are the intents of your questions the same as the implied intents of the examples? If not, then why?

Recognizing Questions at Various Cognitive Levels

Often we find it easy to recognize questions when they are grouped according to particular levels. It is another "ball game" to pick out a particular question type in a "crowd" of questions. Below are some questions for you to consider and identify. Record your judgments and reasons in the spaces provided after this list of questions.

> 1 The Monroe Doctrine was announced about ten years after
>   a. the Revolutionary War.
>   b. the War of 1812.

    c. the Civil War.

    d. the Spanish-American War.

2 An engineer who designs houses is called

    a. a carpenter.

    b. a civil engineer.

    c. an architect.

    d. a draftsman.

3 The main point that our author raises in the story is that

    a. people are self-centered.

    b. people are striving to improve interpersonal relations.

    c. people don't understand human nature.

    d. people are basically good.

4 X and Y can do a piece of work together in 14 days. They work for 6 days; then X quits and Y finishes the work alone in 20 more days. In how many days can Y do the piece of work alone? Show your work below.

5 If you are going to go to the beach to bathe in the sun, but you wish to avoid getting a severe sunburn, you need to avoid the sun in the middle of the day, from 11 AM to 1 PM. The reason that the sun causes more severe burns during this time is because

    a. we are slightly closer to the sun at noon than in the morning or afternoon.

    b. the noon sun will produce more "burn" than the morning sun.

    c. our body chemistry changes as the day proceeds.

    d. the atmosphere changes in gas composition as a result of the heat of the sun.

6 As you consider the behavior of the various ruling members of the tribe, what major assumptions can you make about human behavior?

7 Create a recipe for a new cake dessert.

8 Devise a way in which the traffic problem in your city might be solved.

9 As you consider the characteristics of this type of plastic, which method of molding would be the most effective?

10 Mr. Arthur's painting can be described as
   a. leading the field in modern art.
   b. a proper representation of modern art.
   c. an excellent example of line composition.
   d. an average work with regard to color use.

11 Discuss the central reason for world cooperation on the food problem.

12 Categorize the music you have just heard.

13 As you consider the solutions to the problems that have been suggested, indicate which solution is the most powerful.

14 Compare your use of language in the class with your use of language in a "game" situation.

15 In light of your problem focus, outline the steps you would take in designing an experiment.

Record Your Judgments

Question 1: The cognitive level is _____,
and my reason for this judgment is _____
_____ .

Question 2: The cognitive level is _____,
and my reason for this judgment is _____
_____ .

Question 3: The cognitive level is _____,
and my reason for this judgment is _____
_____ .

Question 4: The cognitive level is _____,
and my reason for this judgment is _____
_____ .

Question 5: The cognitive level is _____,
and my reason for this judgment is _____
_____ .

Question 6: The cognitive level is _____,
and my reason for this judgment is _____
_____ .

Question 7: The cognitive level is _____,
and my reason for this judgment is _____
_____ .

Question 8: The cognitive level is_____,
and my reason for this judgment is_____
_____ .

Question 9: The cognitive level is_____,
and my reason for this judgment is_____
_____ .

Question 10: The cognitive level is_____,
and my reason for this judgment is_____
_____ .

Question 11: The cognitive level is_____,
and my reason for this judgment is_____
_____ .

Question 12: The cognitive level is_____,
and my reason for this judgment is_____
_____ .

Question 13: The cognitive level is_____,
and my reason for this judgment is_____
_____ .

Question 14: The cognitive level is_____,
and my reason for this judgment is_____
_____ .

Question 15: The cognitive level is_____,
and my reason for this judgment is_____
_____ .

Answers to the Sample Questions

Before providing the answers to the previous questions, we need to emphasize that the cognitive level of
questions asked in isolation may be misclassified, for the level
is partly determined by the context in which the question is
raised as well as the intent of the question. For instance, a
question asking for a student to indicate that he understands
what he has read may be coded as comprehension. However,
for this particular student, the question may be an analysis
question, for he may not have read any secondary sources in
which the main ideas were presented. Therefore, he would
have to process primary documents or engage in some
experimentation in order to arrive at the answer.

As you read the answers, remember that the cognitive level given indicates the ideal cognitive intent of the question, but its cognitive level could be different depending upon the situation in which it is phrased and the background information the student brings to the situation. Also, the reason for your judgment may not be identical to the one mentioned. That is all right if you think your judgment is sound based on the information you are considering.

Question 1:
  Cognitive Level *Knowledge*
      Reason: The question is asking for recall of specific fact.
Question 2:
  Cognitive Level *Knowledge*
      Reason: The question is asking for knowledge of classifications of activities.
Question 3:
  Cognitive Level *Comprehension or analysis*
      Reason: The question could be asking for main ideas which the author has made obvious, or the question could be asking for a basic assumption or hypothesis which students only obtain through analysis of specific elements in the writing.
Question 4:
  Cognitive Level *Application*
      Reason: The question is asking the student to apply a principle of problem solving.
Question 5:
  Cognitive Level *Application*
      Reason: The question is asking the student to apply a principle of natural science in order to select the right response.
Question 6:
  Cognitive Level *Analysis*
      Reason: The question is asking the student to detect the basic assumptions from observation of behaviors.
Question 7:
  Cognitive Level *Synthesis*

> Reason: The question is asking the student to synthesize information to make a unique dessert.

Question 8:
Cognitive Level *Synthesis*
> Reason: The question is asking the student to produce a plan which requires pulling information together in a unique way.

Question 9:
Cognitive Level *Evaluation*
> Reason: The student is asked to judge the appropriateness of a particular method of molding in light of the nature of the material.

Question 10:
Cognitive Level *Evaluation*
> Reason: The question is asking the student to apply criteria to Mr. Arthur's painting in order to make a judgment of its quality.

Question 11:
Cognitive Level *Analysis*
> Reason: The question is asking the student to analyze data and situations in order to identify the central reason for cooperation.

Question 12:
Cognitive Level *Analysis*
> Reason: The student has to analyze the basic components and characteristics of the elements of the music, and then place it into a category.

Question 13:
Cognitive Level *Evaluation*
> Reason: The question is asking the student to apply criteria in order to judge a solution as to its effectiveness.

Question 14:
Cognitive Level *Comprehension—Analysis*
> Reason: If the question is just asking the student to compare as a result of discussions about the use of language in these situations, then the question is at the comprehension level. If the question is requiring the student to investigate language use in these two situations and to record key elements noticed and to make some statements about the way language is used, then the thrust of the question is on analysis.

Question 15:
Cognitive Level *Knowledge—Application*
Reason: If the teacher has spent much time discussing the steps one would take, then the
question's thrust is on the student's recall of
these stages, e.g. knowledge of methodology. If
the teacher has not provided immediate and
detailed discussion on this point, but the
student has to identify the problem focus he has
raised, then he has to apply his knowledge of
procedure to the situation and so indicate the
steps.

Point to remember. Questions at the upper cognitive
levels subsume the lower cognitive levels. For example, a
student responding to an analysis question will, at times, have
to function at the levels of application, comprehension, and
knowledge.

Try Writing Some Questions
on Your Own

If you have not written any sample questions at each
of the cognitive levels, try to do so now. Think of a topic
and write a question relating to it at each cognitive level.
After you have done this, ask yourself if your questions are
really at the cognitive levels you intended. Refer to the
examples in this chapter and to the samples in the test of
recognition. Compare your questions with the samples.
Record your reactions. Indicate what you need to do to
change, or continue to do with regard to writing questions at
the various levels. Get a colleague to react to your questions
and share his or her perceptions.

Activities to Help You Create
Effective Questions

This textbook contains activities through which
students can become engaged in planning, doing, and

assessing their questions. But, many, if not all of these activities, can be utilized also by teachers and teachers-to-be in becoming more skilled in using questions at various cognitive and affective levels and in particular strategies.

For example, in Planning Activity 3 in chapter 4, in-service teachers and prospective teachers can identify their preferences for various types of questions by recording the types of questions they employ in class and also the types of questions to which they usually "perk up" their ears. Just what type of questions are they? Do knowledge questions trigger your response? Or do you enjoy getting involved with questions that call for making a judgment?

In confronting questions in their plans and in materials to be used, teachers and teachers-to-be can determine the cognitive and affective levels of their questions. A record can be kept of good examples of questions at each of the cognitive and affective levels.

Teachers can engage in activities such as Involving Activity 3 in chapter 5 which deals with using particular questioning strategies. In such an activity, the teacher can plan the particular steps of a certain strategy indicating the questions he or she wishes to use. As the teacher identifies the questions and their particular sequences, the rationale for the particular moves can be recorded. In this way, the teacher creates a careful record of his plans and also charts how he is functioning with a particular strategy or level or levels of questioning.

When you are employing questions in the classroom, or in peer-teaching situations, you can video or audio record your questions over a period of time and then upon later analysis record the question types you are using on a profile. This would be similar to Assessing Activity 15 found in chapter 6. Such a profile would provide data on the types of questions you used over time with regard to a particular lesson. This information can prove valuable in determining the degree of your success in meeting your objectives regarding the types of questions planned. Another useful activity for teachers is

Assessing Activity 5, question problem identification, also found in chapter 6. This activity can be put into action by teachers to identify any problems they might be having in their questions and questioning, and it can suggest strategies for correcting the revealed problems.

These activities are useful only for assistance in becoming an effective questioner. Surely, as a teacher assists students with the activities in this textbook, he or she also will gain understanding of and skill in questioning. It is crucial to remember that teachers need to work along with students in developing questioning expertise.

The Right Atmosphere for Questioning

To foster effective use of both cognitive and affective questions by yourself and your students requires a classroom atmosphere conducive to questioning activities.

A major factor relating to a positive classroom atmosphere is freedom. This means that students should be free to raise questions at both cognitive and affective levels, and free to process questions that interest them. It means a teacher accepting students' feelings. Students need to realize that they are free to express themselves, for both the teacher and other students respect their right to raise questions. Such a free classroom environment means that the teacher listens to students and is enthusiastic about working with them as they process their questions. The free atmosphere is where the teacher and other students respect the ideas and concerns that students have. Such respect encourages a wide diversity of questions.

This type of classroom environment is one where the teacher respects students as individuals capable of conducting much of their own learning, of directing many of their investigations. This free environment is one where the teacher provides assistance when needed, and students realize this and don't feel threatened when they do require guidance.

A classroom conducive to effective questioning is one in which all members listen to each other. The teacher listens to the students and their questions; classmates listen as their peers raise questions and concerns. They also listen to their teacher. Such open listening provides information that can be crucial in question formation.

A free atmosphere for questioning is one in which the teacher and fellow students demonstrate that they have confidence in each other. "I am confident that you can ask effective questions and that you will use time wisely. I know you will attend to the questions of others and that you will carefully process data uncovered via questioning."

For effective questions and questioning, the classroom atmosphere also has to be responsive. Responsiveness means that the necessary time and materials are provided for processing questions, whether at the cognitive or affective level. It means that the teacher provides sufficient guidance, psychological support required when students are engaged in working with questions. It means that the instructor schedules formal lessons on questions when such lessons are necessary. It means that the teacher provides needed input for students regarding skills in decision making, for processing information in field study or experimentation. The responsive environment is one which has "high interest" materials and interest centers to trigger motivation. Such an environment also has a teacher and fellow students who offer encouragement when necessary in the use of questions. The right classroom atmosphere is one in which the most significant person, the teacher, motivates, provides encouragement, provides data, provides time for "messing around" with information, demonstrates enthusiasm for the areas of study, freely accepts students as inquiring individuals, maintains adequate information levels and materials for investigation, and overall serves as an exemplar of a person "turned on" with questions.

The free and responsive classroom environment is not without structure; nor does it occur without planning. Indeed, such a classroom requires a great deal of structure

and planning. For students to do "their thing" and to really
be involved with questions at the cognitive and affective
levels means that teachers must map out meaningful encounters and necessary support materials.

Working with Questions
is Continuous

For the last several pages, discussion has centered on
ways to get you, us, to work with questions at the cognitive
levels. You have been given some questions to recognize and
analyze. You have been asked to make judgments. You have
been provided with some activities for improving your questions, for making you an effective exemplar of the
questioner.

But reading these pages and engaging in these activities is
only a necessary, but not a sufficient condition for mastering
questioning or effectively guiding your students to become
effective questioners. Improving your own questions requires
constant attention; you need to experiment continuously
with questions you use to guide student learning. You need
to constantly strive to design appropriate activity for
students to involve them in their questioning.

To become an effective questioner, to maintain appropriate functioning with questions, and to continue to motivate and encourage students to be engaged with questioning
requires constant monitoring of our questions and continuous critiquing of the types of activities we provide our
students. We in education never arrive at the perfect solution
or the perfect question, for our students are forever
changing. And this changing nature of individuals requires
that we be diligent in adjusting our questions to meet individual and unique needs. This is not to say we cannot
become proficient in questioning or skilled in getting our
students "turned on" with questions. Rather it means that
we arrive but only with a small "a". We never arrive com-

pletely with the capital "A." We must keep in mind that we as teachers and teachers-to-be are evolving and so are our students.

CONCLUDING NOTES

In using these examples and key words, you should schedule additional time to practice writing questions at each of these cognitive levels. Have a colleague or fellow student react to your questions. Check your results with the examples supplied. Have you used the same or similar words in beginning your questions? Do you think students, if they reacted to or used your questions, would function at the intended cognitive level?

Working with questions is the only way to improve one's questions. Certainly, we all need to do some reading to gain basic knowledge of questions, but it is in the doing that you can become the skilled questioner and the skilled facilitator of student's questions. The principle of doing also applies to students in the classroom and educators should provide the time and assistance required for students to "do" with questions rather than to "talk a good game" regarding questions. One might say that this entire text is designed to enable students to get into the "doing" so that they can gain expertise through experience in questioning.

The next chapter directs the reader's attention to the affective domain and develops affective questions in a manner similar to the technique for cognitive questions forming this chapter.

NOTES

[1.] Condensed from BENJAMIN S. BLOOM, *Taxonomy of Educational Objectives: Handbook I. The Cognitive Domain* (New York: David McKay Co., 1956) pp. 201–207.

[2.] JAMES A. BANKS and AMBROSE A. CLEGG, JR., *Teaching Strategies for the Social Studies* (Reading, Massachusetts: Addison-Wesley Publishing Co., 1973), p. 136. (Some of these key words have been taken from this source, others have been suggested by this author.)

3. O. L. DAVIS, JR., and FRANCIS P. HUNKINS, *Asking About the U.S.A. and Its Neighbors* (New York: American Book Company, 1971) p. 77.

4. BANKS and CLEGG, *Teaching Strategies*, p. 137.

5. Ibid., p. 139.

6. BLOOM, *Taxonomy*, pp. 158–59.

7. BANKS and CLEGG, *Teaching Strategies*, p. 141.

8. Ibid., p. 143.

9. Ibid.

3

Questions in the Affective Domain

This chapter considers questions at several affective levels. Even though this book has separated the two domains, in reality they cannot be divided precisely, for students cannot process information without some emotional response. For example, learners reacting to comprehension questions might be expressing a willingness to respond to the material or valuing some conclusions derived from information. Students organizing information into a value system must function also at cognitive levels of analysis and synthesis. Of course, certain questions can emphasize particular domains as well or levels within the domains.

Affective questions representing all levels should be present in class dialogue, although not all levels need to be utilized in any particular lesson. Just as the teacher schedules cognitive questions to stimulate students to process information with the final goal of generating conclusions or formulating generalizations and then evaluating them, the teacher employing affective questions also wishes to elicit

61

affective responses from learners requisite to some type of value system which can then become part of their daily functioning.

The questions in this chapter represent some exemplars of questions at the several levels of the affective domain. In teaching, you must be conscious that both domains act concurrently. In planning, you can zero in on a particular domain, but you must be cognizant that the other domain also is functioning to some degree.

AFFECTIVE DOMAIN OF THE TAXONOMY OF EDUCATIONAL OBJECTIVES[1]

Receiving (Attending)

At this level the learner is sensitized to the existence of certain phenomena and stimuli; he or she is made willing to receive or attend to them. This is the first and crucial step if the student is to be properly oriented to learn what the teacher has planned.

Receiving has three subsections.

AWARENESS. Awareness is almost a cognitive behavior. But unlike knowledge, the first level of the cognitive domain, the concern is not really with memory or the ability to recall, but that given the appropriate opportunity, the learner merely will be conscious of something and will attend to a situation, phenomenon, object, or stage of affairs.

WILLINGNESS TO RECEIVE. This second stage centers on getting the individual willing to notice a given stimulus, not to avoid it. Will he willingly react to data, situations presented in learning situations?

CONTROLLED OR SELECTED ATTENTION. The third level of receiving is concerned with the differentation of a given stimulus into figure and ground at a conscious or perhaps semiconscious level. This level specifically is asking the student to regulate his perception and to "shut" out distracting stimuli.

Responding

The concern at this level goes beyond merely attending to the phenomenon. At this stage, the teacher desires the child to become involved sufficiently in his work so that he will continue it minus guidance and formal class structure. This level also has three subdivisions.

ACQUIESCENCE IN RESPONDING. At this stage the teacher wants students to comply with a particular situation. This suggests encouraging a certain degree of student passivity so far as the initiation of the behavior is concerned. Compliance might be a better term, for there is more of the element of reaction to a suggestion and less of the implication of resistance or yielding unwillingly.

WILLINGNESS TO RESPOND. The capacity for voluntary activity is the key here. There is the implication that the learner is sufficiently committed to exhibiting the behavior not just because of a fear of punishment, but "on his own" or voluntarily.

SATISFACTION IN RESPONSE. This third stage gets at the feeling the student attains from responding to a question, a situation, or some type of material. It refers to reaction that causes a feeling of satisfaction, an emotional response, generally of pleasure or enjoyment.

Valuing

This third level refers to a thing, phenomenon, or behavior that has worth. The main thrust here is to get the individual to value so that his or her resulting behavior is sufficiently consistent and stable to have the characteristics of a belief or an attitude.

An important aspect of behavior characterized by valuing is that it is motivated not by the desire to comply or obey, but by the individual's commitment to the underlying value.

ACCEPTANCE OF A VALUE. At this level, we are concerned with ascribing worth to a phenomenon, behavior, object, etc. The term "belief" adequately describes what may be thought of as the dominant characteristic here.

One of the distinguishing characteristics of this behavior is consistency of response to the class of objectives, phenomena, etc., with which the belief or attitude is identified.

PREFERENCE FOR A VALUE. Behavior at this level implies not just the acceptance of a value to the point of being willing to be identified with it, but that the individual is sufficiently committed to the value to pursue it, to seek it out, to desire it.

COMMITMENT. Belief at this level involves a high degree of surety; it suggests conviction. In some instances it may border on faith, in the sense of it being a firm emotional acceptance of a belief upon admittedly nonrational grounds.

The person displaying such behavior is clearly perceived as possessing the value in that he acts to further the thing valued in some way, to extend the possibility of his developing it, and to deepen his involvement with it and with the things representing it. He attempts to convince others and to convert them to his cause.

Organization

As an individual successively internalizes values, she encounters situations in which she must (a) organize the values into a system, (b) determine the interrelationship among them, and (c) establish the dominant and pervasive ones. Such a system is built gradually, subject to adjustment as new values are incorporated.

CONCEPTUALIZATION OF A VALUE. This first subcategory allows the individual to create an abstraction or abstractions relating to the values she possesses. Here the individual functions at the level of conceptualization. She is attempting to clarify values identified and found useful into some manageable system.

ORGANIZATION OF A VALUE SYSTEM. Objectives properly classified here are those which require the learner to synthesize a complex of values, possibly disparate ones, and to organize them into an ordered relationship with one another. Here the student is attempting to take identified values and incorporate them into a system for regulating further reactions and actions.

*Characterization by a Value
or Value Complex*

At this level of internalization the values already exist in the individual's value hierarchy and they are organized into some kind of internally consistent system. The individual already has utilized values to regulate his behavior, and he functions quite calmly with these values unless his values are challenged or he is threatened for his views. This level has two substages.

GENERALIZED SET. This level gives an internal consistency to the system of attitudes and values that the individual has synthesized. It enables the person to respond selectively at a very high level. It is sometimes spoken of as a determining tendency, an orientation toward phenomena, or a predisposition to act in a certain way. The generalized set may be considered closely related to the idea of an attitude cluster, where the commonality is based on behavioral characteristics rather than the subject or object of the attitude. A generalized set allows the individual to simplify and order the complex world about him and to act consistently and effectively in it.

CHARACTERIZATION. This final level is the zenith of the internalization process and includes broad objectives relating to the phenomena covered and to the range of behavior comprised. Here we find those objectives which concern a person's view of the universe or philosophy of life. The objectives at this level are so encompassing that they tend to characterize the individual almost completely.

Before considering question examples you may find it useful to compare the levels of the affective domain with those of the cognitive domain.

COGNITIVE DOMAIN[2]	AFFECTIVE DOMAIN[3]
KNOWLEDGE	**RECEIVING (ATTENDING)**
Knowledge of Specifics	Awareness
Knowledge of Ways and Means of Dealing with Specifics	Willingness to Receive
Knowledge of the Universals and Abstractions in a Field	Controlled or Selected Attention

COGNITIVE DOMAIN	AFFECTIVE DOMAIN
COMPREHENSION	RESPONDING
Translation	Acquiescence in Responding
Interpretation	Willingness to Respond
Extrapolation	Satisfaction in Response
APPLICATION	VALUING
ANALYSIS	
Analysis of Elements	Acceptance of a Value
Analysis of Relationships	Preference for a Value
Analysis of Organizational Principles	Commitment
SYNTHESIS	ORGANIZATION
Production of a Unique Communication	Conceptualization of a Value
Production of a Plan, or Proposed Set of Operations	Organization of a Value System
Derivation of a Set of Abstract Relations	
EVALUATION	CHARACTERIZATION BY A VALUE OR VALUE COMPLEX
Judgments in Terms of Internal Evidence	Generalized Set
Judgments in Terms of External Criteria	Characterization

Scanning the two listings will reveal similarities between the knowledge level and the receiving level. The analysis stage and the organization stage have commonalities. Certainly, in order to conceptualize their values individuals must engage in analysis of key elements and determine relationships existing among those elements. Organization of a value system and analysis of organizational principles require similar functioning. The level of synthesis, specifically, the production of a proposed set of operations, has a great deal in common with the characterization stage. To make precise linkages between the two domains is not the point; rather, the central focus is for the teacher to realize that when generating questions in one domain, he or she is also stimulating responses and questions in the other domain.

QUESTIONS AT THE RECEIVING (ATTENDING) LEVEL

The first level of the affective domain is receiving and it has three subdivisions; the first is *awareness*. Questions at this level closely resemble questions at the knowledge level, but the purpose of these questions is to determine if in fact the pupil has been attending to various stimuli, does he have interest in some topic of concern to cause him to pay attention? Given particular situations, will the individual attend or ignore them? Consider the following examples. Do you ask such questions? Have you incorporated similar questions in your lesson plans?

Examples

I have some pictures here of famous people. Look at these pictures and tell me who they are.

Listen to these records of music. Identify the record that is a blend of classical and country music.

Indicate what profession the following people are in.
Billy Graham
Sam Ervin
Barbara Streisand
Paul Newman

Benjamin Spock
David Rockefeller

Study these examples. At first glance, they appear quite similar to questions asked at the knowledge level, but these questions have a different focus and are phrased differently for a specific reason. They are advanced not to determine what the student knows, but to ascertain the areas of knowledge in which the individual is interested.

TEACHER ACTIVITIES

Try writing some examples of your own. Compare them to those in this book.

Willingness to receive is the second subcategory of receiving, and questions at this level aim at determining if the student has a preference for and is willing to commit attention to the topic or task at hand. Will the student make an effort to pay attention, or will he or she seek to ignore the question and the topic to which it refers? Study the examples provided.

Examples

Of the following five activities, which would you prefer to do first?

In our group planning today, I have listed several books we can consider. Indicate on the paper your reaction to each book.

If you had a free afternoon, which of the following activities might you do?

Play ball   _____

Take a nap   _____

Visit a museum _____

Go boating   _____

Read a book   _____

TEACHER ACTIVITIES

React to these examples. Basically, they center on assessing whether individuals will bother with various aspects of learning activities.

Try writing some examples of your own. How do yours compare? Remember to keep a written record of the questions you develop.

The last subcategory of receiving is *controlled or selected attention,* and such questions focus on having the student direct his energies to some specific task endpoint. These questions ask learners if they are willing and able to zero in on specific stimuli. Note that the questions not only ask for particular verbalization but require students to indicate their views and to delineate behaviors in which they engage.

In this domain, questions request students to reveal behaviors which are indicators of affective stances rather than posing questions aimed at some intangible such as degree of pleasure or willingness to respond. The first two examples below ask for statements of agreement or disagreement or for an indication of behavior in which one would or would not engage.

Examples

Mr. Alexander stated in the news broadcast the other day on closed circuit television that he was in favor of raising the level of the dam. He indicated several reasons for his views and these are included in the handout. Designate whether you strongly agree or disagree with the views listed.

Which of the following activities do you usually do, rarely do, never do?

Water skiing

Dancing

Talk with people from backgrounds different from yours

Go to church
Listen to classical music
Visit museums

Read the following questions and put a *y* if your response is *yes*, an *n* if your response is *no,* and an *x* if you have no major reaction.

Would you like to visit a foreign country? _____

Are you willing to do some background reading to understand groups of people who are culturally different from you? _____

Is there a special way in which you like to relax? _____

Would you be willing to listen to a person who was speaking against something you valued? _____

The main thrust of these questions is to reach the aspect of controlled or selected attention. The questions are not designed just to determine random reaction to situations or information, but rather to discover if an individual is willing to attend consciously to various phenomena. Try writing some examples of your own.

Receiving (Attending) Questions— Key Words and Phrases

It seems to be easier to recognize affective question types by beginning phrases rather than individual words. Phrases that seem to start questions at the receiving level are provided below. By no means is this an exhaustive list.

Are you aware	Do you appreciate
Have you heard	Do you recognize
Will you accept	Have you ever
Do you know	Would you like
Do you prefer	Are you interested
Indicate whether	Is there a

QUESTIONS AT THE LEVEL
OF RESPONDING

Like the previous major category, responding has three sub-divisions, the first being *acquiescence in responding*. Questions at this level are geared to determining a student's willingness to respond to some stimuli, even though he might not seek them initially. Such questions seek to identify these concerns and areas of learning that the learner will at least tolerate. The following examples are really asking if one would comply or do something with a little urging. The individual might never volunteer to do these things, but if someone asked, he would agree to participate. Some examples follow.

Examples

Of the following Saturday activities, which do you do with only a little nudging?

Washing dishes

Taking care of little brother

Reading a book

Doing homework

Consider the following two situations: Mr. Jones helping his neighbor move into a new house and Mr. Johnson arranging a drive to raise money for the school library. In which activity would you like to become involved?

Suppose a friend of yours is making fun of someone because his religion is different from hers. Indicate what your reaction would be.

I would ignore the entire situation   _____

I would tell my friend that she should try to
be nice to all people   _____

I would probably join in on the fun making _____

I would get a new friend   _____

TEACHER ACTIVITIES

Analyze these examples. What are their major

features, their common characteristics? Try developing some examples of your own.

The next set of examples refers to questions at the second sublevel of responding, *willingness to respond.* These questions seek to discover if the learner is sufficiently motivated to action or reaction. Would the individual do some particular action voluntarily? If given the opportunity for choice, would he proceed in a particular way?

Examples

In this next section of the unit, you may select from among the five major activities the one on which you wish to work.

Consider how Ms. Arnold acted toward the new persons at the party. Would you be willing to go along with her, not go along with her, or not care either way?

_____

_____

_____

For our school project we need to engage in several activities. Indicate your reaction to the following activities that require doing. Put a *yes* in front of activities you would really like to do, a *no* in front of activities you definitely don't wish to do, an *undecided* in front of activities you have not considered enough, and *either way* in front of those activities about which you have rather neutral feelings.

_____ Do background reading for the project.

_____ Assist in making up the master plan.

_____ Assist in the art support work.

_____ Make the final presentations.

_____ Serve as a critiquer to materials developed.

_____ Help to edit materials.

The teacher can obtain a verbal indication of an individual's willingness to respond, but whether he or she actually does respond cannot be determined by listening to or reading an answer, but only via observation of interaction with a particular situation, content, or other individual. This is important to remember when dealing with the affective domain; it is the behavior of an individual over time that really indicates the mesh between verbalization and actual behavior. Many students have learned to "psyche" out the teacher and reiterate a response appropriate for approval or reward.

TEACHER ACTIVITIES

Consider writing some examples at this level. Compare your questions to the examples. Also think of ways in which you could test whether students really were responding or just "giving you what you want."

The last level of responding is *satisfaction in a response*, and questions at this level are geared to getting some "reading" of whether in fact a person obtains some enjoyment from responding to or dealing with certain content areas, specific topics or situations. As one example indicates, questions relating to music can represent this level. The second examples show that many of our brainstorming activities are really eliciting or have the potential to elicit affective reactions from students. The challenge for us is to "read" the affective responses of individuals as well as to be skilled in posing such questions.

Examples

Listen to this song and record how it first "hits" you.

From our brainstorming activities, indicate those things you would like to do again.

In reading a novel indicate with a *1* those aspects that really appeal to you, a *2* those aspects that have minimal appeal, and a *3* those aspects that elicit negative reactions.

_____ Having exciting characters.

_____ Having a high degree of suspense.

_____ Having a carefully developed plot.

_____ Having a surprise conclusion.

_____ Having a great amount of sadness.

_____ Having both heroes and heroines.

_____ Having a great deal of dialogue.

When observing a painting, indicate with a *yes* those aspects of the painting that have great appeal to you, indicate with a *no* those qualities that cause you to dislike a painting, and indicate with a *neither*, those aspects that really don't elicit any reaction.

_____ The use of bright colors.

_____ The use of abstractions.

_____ The use of vivid realism.

_____ The use of subdued colors.

_____ The unusual blending of reality, as in surrealism.

_____ The use of the human form.

_____ The stress on landscapes.

TEACHER ACTIVITIES

Study these examples and record your own affective responses to them. Which questions would you use in your classroom; never use in your classroom? Ask yourself why you have the affective response you have.

Try to focus on the characteristics of these questions. What do they have in common?

Questions at the Responding Level — Key Words or Phrases

Again, phrases seem to be more helpful to teachers and prospective teachers in recognizing questions at this particular affective level. Some identifying phrases are:

Are you willing   Have you contributed
Do you observe   Will you accept
Do you do   Does it feel pleasant
Have you ever   Are you satisfied
Do you practice   Do you like
Are you interested in   Indicate which
Record how

VALUING QUESTIONS

Questions at this level are concerned with asking if individuals accept a value, have a preference or a commitment to a value or set of values.

Examples for the first division of valuing, *acceptance of a value,* follow. Note that often the value is only implied in the question.

Examples

In *The Taming of the Shrew,* which character did you enjoy the most?

As a result of seeing the movie, explain whether or not you became interested in the problem presented.

Following are some words which can be applied to school. Place a check anywhere along the line toward the word that indicates how you feel about school in general.

School

1. fun   _:_ _:_ _:_ _:_ _:_ _:_ a drag
2. pleasant   _:_ _:_ _:_ _:_ _:_ _:_ unpleasant
3. doing   _:_ _:_ _:_ _:_ _:_ _:_ sitting
4. bad   _:_ _:_ _:_ _:_ _:_ _:_ good
5. dull   _:_ _:_ _:_ _:_ _:_ _:_ bright
6. deep   _:_ _:_ _:_ _:_ _:_ _:_ shallow
7. inquiring _:_ _:_ _:_ _:_ _:_ _:_ telling
8. clear   _:_ _:_ _:_ _:_ _:_ _:_ vague

The last example is in the format of a semantic differential. This relates to a method of observing and measuring the psychological meaning of phenomena. In this case, it is used to get a "reading" on the level of an individual's acceptance of values relating to school. The item is really a series of bipolar words arranged along a continuum. To prevent a person from "psyching" out the item, not all the "good" words are on the left. For example, the first three words indicate "good" in most instances, while the fourth and fifth words indicate some bad aspects of school.

TEACHER ACTIVITIES

Try writing some examples of affective questions at this level. Get a "reading" on your affective response to these types of questions as you create them. Record your examples in your notes. By this time, your notebook should have quite a few examples of questions at various cognitive and affective levels.

Preference for a value is elicited by questions requiring the learner to identify her favored choice either through a statement of or listing of activities in which she actually engages. Such questions not only require a verbalization of "I value this", but request that the learner indicate openly her preference and make efforts to attain the behavior couched in the identified value.

Examples

Of the following activities, which would you prefer to do first?

Read a book   _____

Solve a mathematics problem _____

Go on a field study   _____

Which person would you most wish to be like?

Martin Luther King   _____

Edward Kennedy   _____
Barbara Streisand   _____
Gloria Steinem   _____

A friend of yours disagrees with the rest of your group about something. Which of the following should he do?
a. He should let the judgment of the group prevail.
b. He should make an attempt to get the group to see his viewpoint.
c. He should change to a different group of friends.
d. He should pretend to go along with the judgment of the group.

Indicate whether you agree or disagree with the following statement.

People who do not like the manner in which the United States government is run should either refrain from criticism or leave the country.

Agree   _____
Disagree   _____
Not sure   _____

Explain your reaction.

As can be observed, the treatment of the value is somewhat indirect. The student is not really asked to state which value he prefers, but his response to an item will indicate his value preference. Now it's your turn to write some examples.

At the final level of valuing, *commitment,* questions query individuals as to whether they hold a firm emotional acceptance for a belief, a position, or a mode of operation. These inquiries often are posited to determine if individuals engage in activities indicative of their clearly holding a particular value or value set. Perhaps you recognize some of your questions in the examples provided.

Examples

Identify any "helping others" behaviors which you have engaged in at least three times in the past week.

Read the following paragraphs and indicate with which

views you agree.

Should the press be allowed to publish criticisms of an elected government official? Give the reasons for your response.

You are walking home from work and see several people damaging a statue in a park. Indicate which of the following you would do:
a. Attempt to physically stop the persons involved.
b. Call the police.
c. Just ignore the action.
d. Get other passersby to restrain the people.
e. Inform them that they are being inconsiderate as well as violating the law.

From your analysis of these examples, you may begin to realize that the distinctions between the questions at the various levels of valuing are of degree rather than kind. Teachers need to ask themselves what the intents are of their questions. Questions aimed at preference really differ from questions aimed at assessing commitment from the standpoint of intent. Distinctions in intent can be fine-line and often difficult to discern.

Valuing Questions—
Key Words or Phrases

Valuing questions often begin by asking the individual if he has done something or if he accepts or agrees with something he has encountered in school or out of school.

Do you like	Are you loyal to
Do you feel responsible for	Do you accept
Have you become interested	Do you agree
Have you started	Identify those
Do you participate actively	Rank order
List which	
Defend your stance	Should the

QUESTIONS AT THE
ORGANIZATION LEVEL

These questions probe individuals' responses about whether they are in a sense putting their emotional framework in order. Questions at the first sublevel, *conceptualization of a value,* are really demanding that students identify and classify concepts, especially normative concepts. As indicated in the beginning of this chapter, these questions are extremely close to questions at the cognitive level of analysis. In fact these affective questions are assisting students to conceptualize their values into a more conscious structure.

In the first example below the question requires the student to identify values encountered with values held. Certainly, the respondent must determine relationships among and between concepts held and distinguish those concepts which are normative or value laden, (e.g. honesty) from those that are primarily classificatory or descriptive of reality (e.g., a mountain).

Examples
_____

Observe the following filmstrip and indicate those values that agree with values you hold.

Of the several characters in the story, which ones possess basic assumptions similar to those which you hold regarding the democratic way of life?

Should a senator consider the opinions and concerns of individuals who only represent minority views?

_____ Yes

_____ No

_____ Not sure

Explain your response.

Assume you have an atheist friend staying the weekend with you. On Sunday, which of the following should you do?

_____ Go to church and leave your friend at home.

_____ Try to convince your friend to accompany you to church.

_____ Stay home from church that Sunday.

_____ Have your friend wait outside the church during the service.

TEACHER ACTIVITIES

Analyze the examples for their common characteristics. What about the intent of the questions? What information can you obtain from analyzing the wording of the questions? Write some questions of your own and compare them with the examples. Put your examples in a notebook for later analysis.

Questions relating to the second sublevel of organization, *organization of a value system,* again reflect the close relationship between organization and analysis in that organization of a value system is very similar to the analysis of relationships and organizational principles.

Examples

Please explain why you believe people must be humane when dealing with the poor of other countries.

In viewing the videotape of your reactions yesterday, what are some of your current limitations in dealing with the situation encountered?

In observing the painting "The Night Watch" by Rembrandt, would your reaction to it be most characterized by

a. an admiration of the technique.

b. a check for accuracy regarding the interpretation of the particular period in history.

c. a feeling of awe at the magnificence of man.

d. a reaction as to its wealth on the current market.

When listening to the song "America," which option best
explains your reaction?
a. a feeling of pride.
b. a feeling of responsibility.
c. a feeling of humility.
d. a feeling of thanksgiving.

TEACHER ACTIVITIES

Study the examples and write some of your own.
Remember that the thrust of these questions is to
have the student bring together a complex of values
in such a way that they form an ordered relationship.
The questions should trigger this organizing activity
so that the student brings into consciousness the
values he holds and how they all "tie together."

Organizational Questions— Key Words or Phrases

Questions at this level often commence with words
querying if an individual has done something, suggested some
action, developed a plan, drawn some conclusions or made
some judgment. Again, these questions could be considered
as analysis questions with an emphasis on a value dimension.
Thus many of the key words suggested in chapter 2 for
analysis questions could be used also as indicators for questions at this affective level. In addition to those words, the
following are suggested.

Have you judged	Do you agree
Have you related	In your own words
Does the statement imply	As you view
Have you weighed alternatives	In your opinion
Please explain	

QUESTIONS AT THE LEVEL OF CHARACTERIZATION BY A VALUE OR VALUE COMPLEX

Questions calling for characterization by value really need to be grappled with continually and directed to demonstrate behavior rather than just verbal responses. Questions at the first level of this major division relate to *generalized set* and focus on whether students have internal consistency with their system of attitudes and values at any particular moment. Queries are posited to ascertain the students' orientation toward some phenomena. Inquiries are phrased to isolate persons' predispositions to act in particular manners. Of course, in addition to posing questions the teacher can design situations or simulations in which students must demonstrate via their actions and responses whether indeed they have organized their values into a behavior syndrome to a degree sufficient to cause a consistency of behavior.

Questions at this highest level often ask a person to take a stand and indicate specifically what he or she would do and further to suggest appropriate actions for others as well. In this way, such questions have some commonality with those at the cognitive levels of synthesis and evaluation.

As indicated by the following examples, these questions often are couched in descriptions of situations to which an individual must respond.

Examples

With regard to military aid to foreign countries, which of the following guidelines would you advocate for our nation?

_____ a. Only provide aid to those countries that support our foreign policies.

_____ b. Provide aid to any country that can pay the price for arms.

_____ c. Not provide any aid to foreign countries.

_____ d. Provide military aid to those countries
that will allow for balance of power
among the free world countries.

People are collecting money and supplies for the victims of
the natural disaster that occurred in our state. Consider
privately what you will do to help these people.

A classmate of yours has just arrived in this country from a
non-English speaking country. Her difficulty in speaking English is making it hard for her to make friends.
Which of the following would you do?

_____ a. Leave her alone until she learns more
English.

_____ b. Invite her to your house to visit.

_____ c. Introduce her to your group of friends.

_____ d. Tell her that she should find her own
friends.

TEACHER ACTIVITIES

These questions are really requesting the student to
get all of his values together in order to respond.
Write some examples of your own. Do they have the
potential to get students to organize their values into
meaningful relationships?

The major goal of the affective domain is that the individual will be able to incorporate his affective stances into
recognizable behavior and be willing to engage in such behavior. The individual knows how to relate to this world on
both a cognitive and affective or emotional level and uses his
knowledge in these domains to regulate his interactions with
others and himself.

The final level of the affective domain is *characterization*. This is the zenith of the internalization process in
which all values and value stances, as well as emotional reactions, are organized into varied systems which enable the
individual to function effectively in different situations. In
one sense, the characterization level is where the individual

defines his philosophical orientation to life and responds according to his particular orientation. An individual's response to questions at this level is so broad in a sense that it tends to reveal the overall essence of the individual. The e individual is characterized by what he says, what he does, and how he feels towards his world. Usually these questions only give us indications of the type of student we have rather than a precise quantification of what this person is or is not.

Examples

Of the following goals relating to life, indicate those for which you would strive.

Which of the following beliefs would you say is the most effective in relation to your life and to the lives of your close acquaintances?

Which of the following statements indicate basically what you believe to be the primary purpose of your life?

_____ Relating to your family.

_____ Knowing about your God.

_____ Being able to obtain happiness.

_____ Contributing to the welfare and happiness of others.

_____ Gaining a position of power.

_____ Achieving security for yourself and family.

_____ Being able to change with the times.

This level of the affective domain is a goal that we strive for and have some direct and indirect ways of influencing. However, individuals arrive at this level through interactions not only with school experiences, but also with their encounters in all dimensions and institutions of society. Questions posed at this level are not generated so much as to measure whether we specifically have been successful in our teaching as to obtain some indication regarding the total development of an individual with regard to his affective domain. If the individual comes out well in his response to

our questions at this level, this is good, but we cannot be sure
that we have been the sole direct influence. Of course, we
hope we have made some major input to the development of
the characterization level.

Characterization by Value or
Value Complex Questions—
Key Words or Phrases

These questions usually begin by asking the student what
he would do in a situation. In that sense, the questions are
heavily existential, for they are not concerned with having an
individual indicate what others should do in particular situations, but rather what choice he would make in a free choice
situation. This quality is reflected in some of the key phrases
presented below.

Are you willing	How do you feel
Are you confident	Is that just
What would you do	What did you do
Explain how	Is that your philosophy
Will you engage	Which of the following
	Indicate those

Some thoughts on the words:

Skimming the suggested phrases for questions at
several affective levels reveals considerable overlap. It is not
easy to define precisely how questions will begin at various
affective levels. You have to be guided by the context in
which the question is couched. Students also should become
aware of the importance of examining context in order to
gain skill in recognizing the affective questions present in
their interactions with classmates and materials.

WORKING WITH QUESTIONS IN THE AFFECTIVE DOMAIN

The previous pages presented some examples of questions at various affective levels. As with cognitive questions, getting a handle on affective questions requires careful observation and analysis of these question types to determine commonalities and differences. Keep in mind that questions in this domain deal with emotions, interests, values, attitudes, and appreciations. Such questions often can be asked along with cognitive questions in order to determine the affective reactions students are experiencing while processing information. It also is important for students to crystalize their reactions to information being processed or situations being encountered.

Study the Question Types

Review the types of affective questions and on a separate sheet of paper, list the major intents of questions at each level. Indicate the ways in which specific affective questions start. Identify the major features of particular affective questions. Delineate the common features of questions at particular affective levels. Consider how questions may differ in wording even though they are at the same affective level.

Recognizing Questions at Various Affective Levels

Following are some sample questions at various affective levels. React to each question and record your judgments in the section following the samples.

1 Please complete the blanks for either the individual or country.

Statesman	*Country*
President Sadat	_____
Henry Kissinger	_____
_____	France
Pierre Trudeau	_____
_____	German Federal Republic

2 Below are some activities to which you are to respond in one of three ways: put a check under column 1 if you perform the activity without having someone tell you to do it; a check under column 2 if you do perform the activity, but only after being reminded or told to do it; or a check under column 3 if you never do the activity.

	Column 1	Column 2	Column 3
Picking up my clothes in my room			
Helping with the dinner dishes			
Taking out the trash			
Doing my home-work			
Helping cut the lawn			

3 Indicate how you feel as you respond to each statement below. For ease of scoring, indicate pleased, displeased, or uncertain.

Reading a book _____

Going to the beach _____

Crying over a sad movie _____

Being scared by a spooky movie _____

Trying to figure puzzles _____

Making things with my hands _____

4 Explain whether or not the summary that our class president has made is an adequate expression of your general opinion regarding population control.

5   If the following options were provided this weekend how would you react?
    A. With great interest
    B. With limited interest
    C. With no interest
       1. Watching television Saturday morning _____.
       2. Reading a book Saturday morning _____.
       3. Helping in the kitchen _____.
       4. Helping in the yard _____.
       5. Going to the movies _____.
       6. Doing nothing but relaxing _____.

6   What is your reaction to the position Ms. Adams has taken regarding the "goodness" of man?

7   In your response to the following questions, indicate your reaction with either yes, no, or uncertain.
Would you like to travel to a distant land to meet the people? _____
Are you interested in learning about various types of dance? _____
Are you willing to work with large groups of people?

8   Some nations have indicated that with the world food shortage, it probably is most humane to let large numbers of people in underdeveloped countries starve to death, for to feed them now would only mean they could stay alive for only a short time and they would increase their numbers. This action of feeding them would only make starvation even worse in the future.
Record your emotional reaction to this position and indicate what you are basing your reaction upon.

9   Indicate philosophically how you feel about the basic goodness of man.

10   Does the position Mr. Jones has taken make you want to be like him?

11   Write a short essay relating how you interpret the role of government with regard to providing services for minorities.

12   Compose two statements that would sum up your outlook on life.

13 Indicate your reaction to the man who says he prays while viewing nature during his golf game.

14 Consider the situation regarding various unions' support of their workers' demands for additional salary increases during a time of inflation. Discuss how you react to their demands in light of your basic philosophy relating to the national economy.

15 Describe your position regarding freedom of speech for those who criticize the government.

Record Your Judgments

Question 1: The affective level is _____,
and my reason for this judgment is _____
_____ .

Question 2: The affective level is _____,
and my reason for this judgment is _____
_____ .

Question 3: The affective level is _____,
and my reason for this judgment is _____
_____ .

Question 4: The affective level is _____,
and my reason for this judgment is _____
_____ .

Question 5: The affective level is _____,
and my reason for this judgment is _____
_____ .

Question 6: The affective level is _____,
and my reason for this judgment is _____
_____ .

Question 7: The affective level is _____,
and my reason for this judgment is _____
_____ .

Question 8: The affective level is _____,
and my reason for this judgment is _____
_____ .

Question 9: The affective level is _____,
and my reason for this judgment is _____
_____ .

Question 10: The affective level is _____,

and my reason for this judgment is _____
_____.

Question 11: The affective level is _____,
and my reason for this judgment is_____
_____.

Question 12: The affective level is _____,
and my reason for this judgment is_____
_____.

Question 13: The affective level is _____,
and my reason for this judgment is_____
_____.

Question 14: The affective level is _____,
and my reason for this judgment is _____
_____.

Question 15: The affective level is _____,
and my reason for this judgment is _____
_____.

Answers to the Sample Questions

Questions dealing with these realms or subrealms
often are more difficult to categorize precisely than questions
in the cognitive domain. This difficulty is due partly to the
nature of the domain, and partly to our lack of experience in
formulating questions in this domain. Also, those questions
requesting a statement or explanation of emotion, an indication of interests, a delineation of values, or an expression and
explanation of attitudes or appreciations also are cognitive to
a certain degree. Earlier in this chapter the two taxonomies
were listed and points of crossover between them indicated.
Keep this in mind as you react to the answers to the samples.
Also, your reasons for deciding on a particular affective level
may differ slightly from the reasons provided on the following pages. However, the samples are classified according to
their major affective intent.

Question 1:
Affective level *Receiving (Attending)*
Reason: This question is designed to test a stu-

dent's awareness of certain information. Has
the student been attending to or receiving particular stimuli? This level of affective question
is almost cognitive, but the thrust of the question is not to measure cognitive understanding,
but to determine if a student has sufficient
interest in something to cause him or her to
attend to it.

Question 2:
  Affective level *Responding*
    Reason: The question's main thrust is to determine
    the response of the individual to certain activi-
    ties. Specifically, the question is designed to
    ascertain the degree of acquiescence in respond-
    ing that the individual has.

Question 3:
  Affective level *Responding*
    Reason: This question is concerned with deter-
    mining the individual's satisfaction in a re-
    sponse. Does the individual enjoy doing the
    things listed?

Question 4:
  Affective level *Valuing*
    Reason: This question is aimed at determining the
    level of commitment to an underlying value
    regarding a particular issue, in the example's
    case, population control.

Question 5:
  Affective level *Receiving (Attending)*
    Reason: This question is concerned primarily with
    determining the level of attention that an
    individual might give to particular activities.

Question 6:
  Affective level *Valuing*
    Reason: This question, requesting a reaction to a
    particular position taken by another individual,
    is really trying to assess the level of acceptance,
    the strength of a belief an individual possesses.

Question 7:
  Affective level *Responding*
    Reason: This question is designed to assess the
    degree of willingness of an individual to respond
    to various situations.

Question 8:

> Affective level *Characterization by a Value or Value Complex*
>
> Reason: The thrust of this question is directed at determining a predisposition to act in a certain way toward the situation. It also has a cognitive component since it asks the person to indicate what he is basing his reaction upon.

Question 9:

> Affective level *Characterization*
>
> Reason: The question is asking the person to respond about her basic view of people. To give an adequate response, the individual has to draw upon the total set of values which she has internalized in her approach to life.

Question 10:

> Affective level *Valuing*
>
> Reason: Specifically, the question is asking the individual if he accepts a value which has been revealed by a particular person.

Question 11:

> Affective level *Organization*
>
> Reason: This question is requesting the person to bring together a complex of values in order to make precise her view relating to the role of government.

Question 12:

> Affective level *Characterization*
>
> Reason: This question is requiring the student to respond from a philosophical position and to draw upon basic beliefs, attitudes, and values.

Question 13:

> Affective level *Organization*
>
> Reason: The question is asking the individual to respond to a particular value stance and to react to it in light of his own value system.

Question 14

> Affective level *Organization*
>
> Reason: This question asks the student to weigh the consequences of a particular action in the general society and to indicate how he or she would respond to it as an individual.

Question 15:
Affective level *Valuing*
Reason: This question is asking for an individual to
reveal his commitment level to the principle of
free speech.

Points to Remember

Sometimes there exists a fine line of distinction
between the levels of organization and characterization. In
essence, questions at the organization level take a narrower
focus, asking the individual to respond to a particular situation and to bring into consideration specific values, attitudes,
emotions, and/or appreciations. The characterization level
asks the student to respond more globally, and requires that
he activate not only one set of values, but several sets, and to
draw upon the interrelationships among these several sets in
order to generate a response.

It should be remembered that the teacher should take
care not to pry with affective questions. These questions are
raised to allow students to become aware of this domain of
their functioning and to understand why they function as
they do, and to realize that they can change the way or ways
in which they function affectively. Affective questions are
designed to make the processing of information and the
learning encounters more complete.

Write Some Examples of Your Own

Hopefully, you tried your skill at writing questions at
the various affective levels as you read the first part of this
chapter. If not, do so here. In one sense, asking you to try
your hand in creating affective questions is an affective question aimed at determining your willingness to respond as well
as your commitment to the value of good affective questions.

To give yourself a "push," consider a situation that has
occured in your classroom or one that you would like to have

happen in your classroom. What questions can you pose that would get at responding, at valuing, at organization? Think of a situation that has occured recently in the news. Jot down some questions you could ask students to get them to consider the value stances and attitudes possessed by individuals, by themselves.

Create some examples. Check them against the examples throughout the first part of this chapter and also the examples contained in the test of recognition. How do you compare? Would you really ask those questions? If given a second chance, which questions would you change? Which questions would you keep as is? Explain the reasons for your responses.

Activities to Help You Write Productive Affective Questions

As mentioned in the previous chapter, this textbook contains many activities for involving students in questioning, but teachers and teachers-to-be also can use these activities to gain skill in using questions at the several affective levels.

Planning Activity 4 in chapter 4 deals with determining the rationale for asking particular questions. Ask yourself some questions in the affective domain, and then query yourself as to why you asked the particular ones you did. Do these questions really reach your feelings, your beliefs, your attitudes? Do your questions get at your appreciations?

Another activity that can be used to check out affective questions is Planning Activity 5 which deals with a panel checkout of questions. Here you can generate questions at any and all levels of the affective domain and have a panel of colleagues or education students (it need not be large) react to your questions to determine if they are on target. You also can serve as a panel member in some situations, which gives you practice in recognizing others' questions as to affective levels.

Role playing is a powerful activity to use with students to get them to experience various situations and ideas. Role

playing also can provide situations in which we pose questions at particular affective levels to determine our affective
responses and those of others. Involving Activity 1, found in
chapter 5, deals with role playing a questioning situation. A
crucial component of role playing is the discussion or debriefing which follows the activity. Find colleagues or fellow
education students who are willing to engage in the role playing and also in the debriefing sessions. Such sessions will not
only improve your affective questions, but will allow you to
obtain a better understanding of your "affective" self.

Involving Activity 4, also in chapter 5, deals with
analyzing questions in various materials. Such an activity will
provide you, the teacher, with practice in recognizing questions at several affective levels. It also allows practice for
self-analysis regarding responses to particular affective questions.

A prime activity for use when dealing with questions in
this domain is Assessing Activity 3, found in chapter 6. This
activity deals with an attitude check on questions. Just what
are your attitudes, your reactions, your dispositions, toward
certain questions? This activity can be most meaningful for
it causes you to examine your reactions to questions and
focuses your attention on your affective realm of functioning.

Matching questions with goals, Assessing Activity 8, also
can be utilized to get a better handle on affective questions.
If you have particular goals for using specific affective questions, do your questions match up with your stated goals?

The above activities are not designed solely for working
with affective questions. But the important point is that we
can use such questions to probe our affective domain of
functioning and thus become more cognizant of the ways in
which we deal with this domain and our affective questions.
Such self-awareness should allow us to work more effectively
with students. The reader is invited to look over quickly
some of the other activities to determine those which may be
helpful in providing practice in using affective questions.

The Proper Atmosphere for Affective Questions

In chapter 2, the appropriate environment for stimulating teacher and student questions at both the cognitive and affective domains was discussed. It was stressed that the environment has to be free, in the sense of letting individuals function without fear of being criticized or ridiculed. The individual must realize his self worth and understand that he has something to contribute. Also the environment has to be responsive in the sense of providing the necessary time, support materials, support individuals, and sufficient educational space.

Additional points exist which one should consider when establishing an environment conducive to the raising, processing, and assessing of both cognitive and affective questions. It is especially important that we as teachers exert care less we suppress development of students' affective questions and responses to such questions by imposing our own opinions. A sure way to stifle the use of and response to affective questions is to let the class know that "only our set of values are considered valid in our classroom." Of course, we usually do not say this verbally, but our actions can relay this message quite effectively.

In assuring the proper atmosphere for affective questions we must provide opportunities for students to share their affective questions and their reactions to such questions. Debriefing sessions can provide for this. Involvement is a crucial part of the free and responsive environment. Students need to confront their questions, others' questions; their ideas and beliefs, and others' ideas and beliefs. Such involvement can foster effective listening.

Even though affective questions deal with emotion, values, beliefs, and appreciations, students must provide some bases supporting their questions and their responses to affective questions. In the conducive classroom environment, the teacher should encourage students to support their reactions

to affective questions with evidence and articulated rationales. Responding to affective questions is not just saying
"well, I just feel that way because."

   When discussing creating the effective classroom environment in chapter 2, we mentioned that the teacher needs to be
a significant other person. Truly, the teacher must be an
exemplar of the asker of quality affective questions. This
requires work on the teacher's part, but it should have good
payoff with regard to students' questions. Students will find
it easier to formulate such questions if they experience such
questions raised by the teacher, and if they grapple with
responding to some of the teacher's affective questions.
Research indicates that students' questions often resemble
teacher's questions. How important is it for us then to ask
meaningful affective questions? A final point to remember is
that a proper environment for "messing" with questions is
one which fosters student enjoyment—enjoyment in asking,
in listening, in challenging, in responding, in being involved.

Working with Questions
is Continuous

   In chapter 2, we asserted that the teacher really never
"arrives" with regard to questions. This is true also regarding
questions in the affective domain. We constantly need to
plan, to experiment with, and to monitor our affective questions, not only to get students to function within this realm
and to assess our effectiveness in stimulating such student
action, but to continue to raise the quality of our affective
questions. Such constant work is necessary for our "clients"
are changing, value bases are being altered in some cases, and
our questions need to reflect these changes. Also, as we learn
more about the realm of questioning in both domains, we
need to make minor, and sometimes major, adjustments in
our questions and questioning techniques.

Our responses to working with questions in both domains will indicate to some extent our affective reactions to questions, to the processing of information, to the role of being the student, to the role of being the teacher.

CONCLUDING NOTES

This chapter has treated various affective questions by presenting examples and description. It also has provided means by which we can work with such questions. It is evident that many of the questions have linkages to the cognitive domain with questions at the organization and characterization levels clearly related to questions at the analysis, synthesis, and evaluation levels.

The teacher must learn to meld questions from both domains, for in the reality of the classroom it is hard to separate them. Students also need to be conscious of both domains so that they not only pose better questions, but that they will also become aware of the emotional dimensions of their learning and their living.

Teachers are not to use affective questions to pry. We must respect peoples' privacy. However, students must be cognizant of their values, their emotional reactions, and their commitment to particular dimensions of life. Affective questions can assist.

NOTES

[1] Copyright © 1964 by the David McKay Company, Inc. From the book *Taxonomy of Educational Objectives, Handbook II— the Affective Domain.* Edited by D. R. KRATHWOHL, B. S. BLOOM, and B. B. MASIA. Reprinted with permission of the David McKay Company, Inc.

[2] BENJAMIN BLOOM, *Taxonomy of Educational Objectives Handbook I, Cognitive Domain* (New York: David McKay Company, Inc., 1956), pp. 201–207.

[3] KRATHWOHL, *Taxonomy,* pp. 176–185.

4

Involving Students in Planning Questions and Questioning Strategies

Students must proceed through three stages when using questions in the classroom: a planning stage, an actual involvement or doing stage, and an assessing stage. In reality, these three stages proceed in a cycle similar to the one represented in Figure 4-1.

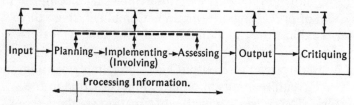

FIGURE 4-1   The Cycle of Student Questioning.

As indicated in the figure, planning, implementing, and assessing activities all relate to processing information.

101

Planning comprises those activities or subprocesses that one does to prepare for some learning encounter or investigation. In chapter 4, the planning activities relate to determining the types of questions to utilize in inquiry, assessing the function of questions, developing schema for the use of questions in specific inquiries, and in general developing plans and steps for mapping out investigations.

Implementing (involving) refers to activities in which students use questions and strategies created in the planning stage. Implementing activities are discussed in detail in chapter 5. At this stage of processing information, students utilize their questions and particular strategies to gain understanding of information and situations. At this point students employ questions to gain handles on their cognitive and affective understandings of information. They also generate additional questions for further inquiry relevant to particular foci. They react to questions which they confront either in materials or in people's dialogue.

The assessing stage is the third major step in processing information. At this juncture, students assess, judge, and evaluate the effectiveness of their own questions and strategies as well as make evaluations of questions found in materials or in the investigations of others. Students engaged in assessing not only focus on their cognitive functioning, but also on their affective functioning. Chapter 6 deals with activities to involve students in this stage of information processing.

As shown in the diagram, these three stages comprise the system of processing information. Combined, these three stages exhibit the function of transformation. Transformation refers to operations that cause input into the system to be transformed into output. Planning, implementing, and assessing require inputs in order to initiate action in the system. The processing of the information via these three stages results in an output or outputs, which are classified as information learned. Notice that after the output there is a critiquing stage. This activity differs from the assessing stage, in that critiquing is concerned with judging the accuracy or usability of the information gained (learned), the output, through the processing of information, while the assessing stage is concerned with judging the effectiveness with which the learner utilized the process as well as the plans for the process. Assessing refers to the quality of the transformation process, while critiquing refers to the quality of the resultant learning. Of course, all of the stages are interrelated. In Figure 4-1, this is depicted by the dotted feedback loop going to all stages. The function of feedback and adjustment is ongoing; that is, the students, when processing information and reacting to conclusions, must continuously monitor what they are doing at each stage and determine if it is satisfactory with regard to their particular learning goals.

This particular chapter responds to the question "How do I get my students involved in planning their questions for the effective processing of information?" The chapter centers on providing the reader with specific activities designed to furnish practice for students in planning questions, generating different kinds of questions, and organizing questions into some type or types of strategies. The situations contained within this chapter are not for the teacher per se; rather, they are things that students can do to plan their use of questions more effectively. In all cases, the activities provide opportunities for students to consider formally the dimensions of planning questions. The activities should provide occasions for the teacher to introduce formal lessons on the question which will enable students to develop conceptual frameworks for questions in both the cognitive and affective domains.

There has been no attempt to state that a particular activity should be used with students of a particular age or grade. Surely, some of the examples in this and following chapters are more appropriate for the secondary level, while others are geared to the elementary level. But regardless of the level at which you assume an example to be, the activities can be utilized across all levels of schooling. Of course, your expectations will vary as to the degree of student sophistication or responses to questions generated, or the degree of student depth of investigation.

But the important point to remember is that students at all levels need to experience situations calling for planning, using, and assessing questions. Children in the primary grades ask questions and do process or should process information. Students at other levels of schooling should also be encouraged to become actively involved in questions and questioning. The reader is invited to adapt the examples in the following chapters to the particular grade level at which he or she works.

Some readers might react to certain activities and indicate that young students cannot be expected to process questions at all of the cognitive levels.. However, the teacher should remember that most primary grade students are in the concrete operational stage, and they can think about phenomena as long as they can tie the phenomena to action and experience them through the senses. Young children will not be highly logical and skilled in processing questions at the upper levels of the taxonomies. Nevertheless, they can become involved at these upper levels. They can look for (analyze) key ideas or major features in their environment. They can suggest (synthesize) solutions to particular problems that are within their sphere of experience.

Questions have difficulty levels as well as cognitive and affective levels. Young children can deal with high-level cognitive and affective questions that are easy. For example, they can be asked to respond to an evaluation question dealing with food, using the criterion of taste. This is a high-level cognitive question, evaluation, but it is of an easy nature. In contrast, students at the secondary level might be asked a question at the lower level of cognitive knowledge, but one which has a high difficulty factor. Such a question might be to recall how the Federal Reserve Board introduces and circulates money in the national market. Also, we need to remember that formal thought begins to be perfected at around eleven years of age.

The goals of thinking are expressed for all levels of education. Thinking requires that questions be raised and answered. Hopefully, readers will accept this view that students at all levels and at all abilities should experience activities with questions at all cognitive and affective levels.

The activities presented in this chapter have a consistent format: a rationale, a general description, a sample of an activity sheet where necessary, an example or examples of the activity used within the context of a specific subject, and in some instances, related information. Thus, the reader will know the basic reason for each activity and have some idea how to employ it within the context of a particular subject. The content examples provided do not exclude one from using other content areas.

To reiterate, this chapter contains activities designed to engage learners in planning the use of questions in or outside the classroom. Activities relating to what the student does with the plans, the actual use of questions, will be the substance of chapter 5.

PLANNING ACTIVITIES

Planning Activity 1: Brainstorming Question Types

BASIC RATIONALE. The prime rationale of this activity is to provide students with opportunities to produce myriad kinds of questions relating to a particular focus. Often in class periods insufficient time is allotted learners to just consider the types of questions possible. Denied adequate time to generate questions for investigation, learners over-rely on the questions of the teacher or gear their inquiry to questions suggested in the materials encountered in the study of a particular lesson.

This activity can get students to assume increased responsibility for their learning—not only the actual asking of questions or responding to questions in materials, but planning means by which they can process information to arrive at meaningful conclusions. In the first chapter, open inductive discovery was mentioned as a means for providing individual experience in a particular process of inquiry. Brainstorming seems to lay a requisite foundation for exploring techniques in how to learn. The activity also can relate to the structured inductive discovery lesson which aims at having learners discover particular concepts of information. The specific type of discovery to which this activity refers depends upon the overall plan of the teacher. (See chapter 7 for more detailed discussion of these modes of discovery.)

Students producing a list of ideas can form many kinds of possible questions prior to an investigation and can discern the value of such questions in focusing their investigation. Additionally, learners can become cognizant of the types of questions they can and do ask and can modify their questions if they identify an overemphasis on questions at lower cognitive levels.

Students cannot brainstorm in a vacuum. They cannot identify question types and the value of such questions without some understanding of questions. Thus, after such a brainstorming session, the teacher may wish to have a formal lesson dealing with types of questions at several cognitive and affective levels. However, the teacher should be careful not to overwhelm the students. Perhaps, in the beginning, formal lessons should only center on a few types of questions at any one time.

THE ACTIVITY. Indicate to the class the importance of questions to any type of investigation, but stress that it takes time to consider the questions they may wish to utilize in research. Therefore, inform the class that you are going to provide ten or fifteen minutes during which they are to generate as many questions as possible about the particular topic of the lesson. They should not try to determine if the questions are good or bad or their cognitive level; rather they should just record queries that come to mind relating to the topic.

After the allotted time, have the students share their questions with classmates to determine the appropriateness of the questions to the topic. Questions can be organized by cognitive level, intent of the questions, or possible directions of investigation they might suggest.

Students can work in teams of two in this brainstrorming activity and record their questions on forms either of their own design or the teacher's. The form might resemble the one depicted here.

Brainstorming Session #_____

TOPIC:

POSSIBLE QUESTIONS

_____

_____

_____

_____

_____

GENERAL REACTIONS TO
QUESTIONS GENERATED

_____

_____

Example. Assume that the teacher wishes students to study the topic of conservation. Before the lesson actually begins and takes a particular tack, the teacher allows the students time to indicate any questions regarding the topic. After the brainstorming, the teacher can indicate that the inquiries suggested should be considered for their worth in directing the student to meaningful investigations and suggestions for a tentative hypothesis.

Brainstorming about the topic of conversation might produce a sheet like this one on conservation.

Brainstorming Session #1

TOPIC: Conservation

POSSIBLE QUESTIONS

What is conservation?

How does conservation affect me?

What are some examples of conservation?

Where do I look for examples?

What did I read about conservation?

What happens in areas where there is no conservation?

What individuals say there is a problem?

How is a problem defined?

How would I check my community for examples of efforts of conservation?

What is the opposite of conservation?

GENERAL REACTIONS TO QUESTIONS GENERATED

Questions should provide me with a definition of conservation. I need to consider some major hypotheses. Perhaps I can test the hypothesis that conservation is necessary.

Note. Of course, the specific sheet will vary with the individuals involved, but the activity has assisted our student, in this case, in delineating questions for investigation.

Initially, some learners will be surprised at the unproductiveness of their questions in leading them to deriving conclusions, while other pupils may be elated by the high cognitive level of their questions. A prime result of the experiment is that learners achieve awareness of their questions and to some degree consciousness of their value bases regarding particular subject matter in the school curriculum. In order to be functional within the process dimension, learners need such cognizance of their functioning; they need to stop and think, "just what am I doing, and what do I consider worth my study time?" Some students have never queried themselves on these points.

Planning Activity 2: Using Reaction Avenues

BASIC RATIONALE. Students need to comprehend that the types of questions generated will influence to a great extent the nature of their answers and the overall direction of the investigation. Appraisal of the consequences on their questions is important, for such awareness provides useful data in determining the worth of a potential direction of inquiry and the productivity of their questions. Also, being cognizant of the consequences of raising particular questions can enable them to plan the type of materials necessary for the quest. Of course, the teacher can use a reaction avenue for planning lessons, but the emphasis here is on students using these avenues in plotting their own investigations.

This particular activity primarily reflects the structured inductive discovery lesson in that the students are to generate questions and to determine the possible directions of investigations, but the purpose of planning activities is to enable them to arrive at a particular concept or understanding. However, the activity could be part of a planning phase of a hypotheticodeductive discovery (See chapter 7 for detailed discussion of this type of discovery) lesson in which the students are provided a major general question or hypothesis and required to delineate the means by which they might test out or apply the central question. The reader should realize that the activities are not locked into any particular discovery mode but possess sufficient flexibility to be used in both inductive and deductive manners.

In order to be successful with creating reactive avenues, the teacher should have provided formal lessons dealing with the types of questions in both domains. Thus, students can use the activity for gaining expertise in developing reaction avenues and also for practicing types of questions encountered formally.

THE ACTIVITY. Indicate to students that it is not only necessary to comprehend how to formulate questions of several types, but that it is also important to determine the directions particular types of questions can take. With regard to a particular lesson topic, allow the class to think of the central question for investigation. After they have recorded it, have them indicate anticipated responses or answers to this central question. What other questions are suggested by this key question? In what potential direction could one proceed in response to this initial inquiry and the accompanying responses? After students have indicated some responses and resulting questions, research could commence. During the topic examination, learners can record additional questions and responses generated, scheduling checkpoints to critique the types of questions employed and determining if the responses are leading in productive directions and toward the desired conclusion.

The teacher should move around the room and work with various student groups offering suggestions regarding possible directions for additional questions. The teacher should, however, encourage the students to ask for guidance rather than accepting information the teacher volunteers. If students seem at a standstill, the teacher could inquire regarding the type of assistance required. Are there any related questions the teacher can raise centering on the topic? Will these questions provide the answers students want? If not, how can they alter the questions to be more productive for their search? Have all major directions of investigation been identified? What is the consensus of the group regarding directions or subtopics for investigation? Are the directions important? Will they provide data to answer the major concern or hypothesis? Learners should also ask themselves such questions as they engage in this planning activity.

 Example. Suppose a teacher has planned a social studies lesson focusing on land use and how people decide to utilize their environment and how the environment influences or limits people's choices. The teacher might have on the board the major question, "What is the Green Valley used for?" Students are to focus their planning on questions they can raise regarding land use in this particular valley. After the planning, students should then use their questions in investigating the specific aspects of this topic in order to formulate a conclusion.

 Following is an abbreviated version of one student's reaction avenue to the central question, "What are the uses of the Green Valley?" Analysis of this example reveals several possible avenues to explore as well as the specific questions and responses.

Reaction Avenue Form

Name: <u>Bonneville</u>

Lesson: <u>Social Studies — Land Use</u>

My Objectives: <u>I will suggest questions at particular levels that will</u>
<u>assist me in analyzing land use in the Green Valley.</u>
<u>My questions should lead to several avenues of</u>
<u>investigation.</u>

Date: _____

(Initiatory Question)

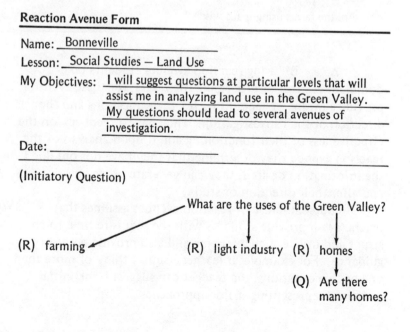

(Q) What type of farming?

(R) Truck Farming   (R) Dairy farming

(Q) How does truck farming in the area compare
     with that of other areas we have studied?

(R) The truck farming is done on smaller acreage.
     The farms specialize in one crop culture.

(Q) What are the major characteristics of such
     truck farming?

(R) The farms use irrigation, employ local workers, and
     have large amounts of machinery.

(Q) Are the farms using space wisely?

Note. By using reaction avenues students take
dominant control of processing their data, for these avenues
provide a means of accounting for their questions and the
direction of their investigation. They have a feedback on the
effectiveness of their functioning and if upon analysis of the
reaction avenue they determine that they have not obtained
the information desired, they can generate other questions
and alter their direction of study.

Of course, the use of reaction avenues assumes that
teachers will provide students with the requisite time to construct and utilize such a scheme and also provide necessary
guidance. For example, if learners cannot think of more than
one or two questions, the teacher can suggest some initial
questions representing major approaches.

Planning Activity 3: Checking
Question Preference

BASIC RATIONALE. Planning Activity 3 can provide
feedback for students regarding the types of questions they
usually ask when considering certain topics, their preference
for asking particular types of questions, and their degree of
knowledge about questions at several cognitive and/or affective levels. In such an activity, students often come to realize
that they really have never inquired of themselves if they
have preferences for certain types of questions or not. They
have never really engaged in any self-diagnosis of their questioning behavior, certainly not as a part of their basic
planning for study.

This activity is concerned not so much with enabling
learners to gain information or to become knowledgeable of
process as it is an attempt at self-analysis relating to a specific
dimension of their behavior. The encounter can provide
learners with some insight about who they are with regard to
their roles as students.

THE ACTIVITY. One way to conduct this activity is to provide time for learners to generate ten questions they would
like to ask about a particular topic. After one listing, have
learners rank order the questions from the most important or
crucial to investigate to the least important. Then have the
class members consider why they gave the questions the
ordering they did and judge if such an ordering is productive
for formulating desired conclusions. Some class members
may discover all of their questions are really related to the
same level of information. Many pupils may realize they are
content just to find out what the author said and accept his
or her conclusion without challenge. Other students may
detect that their questions are not really directing them to
the types of conclusions they intend to deduce from the
topic. "I want to find why people behave as they do, and

yet, I only ask questions that relate to what happened and when; I never pose questions looking for the why."

The rank ordering can be done using the Question Preference form.

Question Preference

___

TOPIC:_____

QUESTIONS I THINK IMPORTANT (DO FIRST)	RANK ORDERING OF QUESTIONS (DO SECOND)
_____	_____
_____	_____
_____	_____
_____	_____
_____	_____
_____	_____
_____	_____
_____	_____

Overall reaction to questions I prefer:

___

Example.   A teacher is having a lesson on recent past events, and students are suggesting topics which they desire to raise questions about. A focus such as the Watergate story and Senate Hearings might be used. If so, the form for question preference might resemble the following survey.

___

TOPIC: Significant Events, Watergate

QUESTIONS I THINK IMPORTANT (DO FIRST)	RANK ORDERING OF QUESTIONS (DO SECOND)
1. How do I feel about the major figures in the investigation?	1

2. How do I feel about the persons
   on the Senate Committee?   6

3. What do I know about the topics
   suggested by the President?   2

4. Why was there conflict between
   the Committee and the President?   4

5. How can we tell if all the witnesses
   were telling the truth?   5

6. What would I do in a similar
   circumstance?   3

7. Could I develop a plan to get
   at the information?   7

Overall reaction to questions I prefer: I seem to prefer questions getting at the overall picture, and questions aimed at determining how I would act.

Note. A variation of this activity would be to have students rank order a ready-made list of questions relating to a particular topic. Learners also might be presented with questions that have concerned certain scholars or important individuals. Students could then determine the relative importance of these questions. It might be productive for learners to realize that even though informed people might posit the same questions regarding some topic or issue, great variance can exist as to the importance they assign these questions.

This activity relates learners' functioning to the affective domain. Certainly the thrust of asking students to identify preferences relates to the affective sublevels of valuing, "preference for a value" and "commitment." In asking individuals to reveal those questions they consider primary, the teacher is asking students to examine their positions regarding specific situations. In the "preference for a value" the focus attempts to determine if the student deliberately examines myriad viewpoints for the purpose of forming some opinions about them.

The activity causing students to rank their questions reveals just what issues or aspects of issues they deem most important. Of course, the students may have to consider more than just ten questions. Also, some class citizens might consider ten questions as loading on the first and second rankings. In other words, they may indicate equal preference on many of their questions. This is fine for at least they are asking themselves just where they stand, what they consider important, what some of their values are, and whether they really exhibit value stances by the questions they pose and consider primary.

Observation of the ranking of the questions may reveal the degree of commitment a person has to certain values. If some queries are consistently down the line in order of preference, then the individual might ask himself just how committed he is to something. The student can't be committed to something if he or she does not pose questions that deal with it.

Planning Activity 4: Question Rationale Check

BASIC RATIONALE. The question rationale check is designed to provide students with a vehicle for determining why they have raised or selected the questions they have. It is intended to encourage learners to be reflective as to the types of questions employed. It is a response to the basic query, "Why did I ask that question?"

This check could be linked to the mode of open inductive discovery for the function is to learn about the process or rather a subprocess of discovery, that is, the question-asking dimension. Students have an opportunity to analyze their questions in their planning. In a sense they are interrogating themselves to identify what they believe important and to ascertain their knowledge of how questions can serve them. It is most important in planning for persons to understand why they formulate the questions they do. In analyzing their questions, people get at that their preferences or values and indeed focus on how they have organized their values into a value system. Usually this is a stage glossed over in classrooms, if it is considered at all.

THE ACTIVITY. The activity consists of simply having class members record questions deemed worthy of investigation. After listing, students prepare a brief oral or written defense of the questions. The defense can be presented to another classmate or to a larger or total class group.

Question Rationale Check Sheet

TOPIC: _____

MY QUESTIONS	MY REASON FOR THIS QUESTION
1._____	_____
	_____
	_____
	_____
2._____	_____
_____	_____
	_____
3._____	_____
_____	_____
4._____	_____
_____	_____

Example. Let's consider a lesson focusing on the Surrealist School of Art of which Salvadore Dali is perhaps the best known representative. Students might be looking at Dali's painting of the Crucifixion depicting a lifelike figure hanging from a modern cross. The teacher might ask the students to list several questions that come to mind as they observe the painting. After they have listed the questions they consider why they raised the queries. A particular class member might develop a sheet like the example here.

Question Rationale Check Sheet

TOPIC: Art — Surrealist Painting, Salvadore Dali, Crucifixion

MY QUESTIONS	MY REASONS
How does Dali get the effect of having the figure suspended in space?	Technique looks interesting
I wonder whom he did the painting for?	Just curious
What are my feelings as I look at the painting?	Interested in my reactions
When was it done?	Just curious as to when this was done
Who is Dali?	Curious

My overall reactions to my questions. My questions are geared to just finding out some facts and also discussing some of my feelings. My initial questions don't seem to get at the purpose for the painting or how he sets the mood.

Note. Most likely, the example provided would not be one for an elementary student but could be appropriate for a secondary student in an art appreciation class.

This activity can be used in conjunction with some of the previous activities in the planning stage, such as brainstorming and the development of reaction avenues. The encounters in this chapter need not be used in isolation or only once, but they can be employed whenever there is a need for such planning.

The thrust of the Rationale Check is on understanding process and also on apprehending self in relation to what the student considers important. For this reason, the affective level of valuing and organization can be emphasized here. This situation is included in planning because it provides learners with information useful for planning questions they might later pose when becoming involved in some subject area.

Planning Activity 5: Panel
Check-Out of Questions

BASIC RATIONALE. Oftentimes students require opportunities to obtain others' reactions to their questions, for peer perceptions bring additional insights to their questioning behavior. It is essential in the planning phases, especially when learners are first becoming acquainted with good questions and questioning techniques, for students to try out questions on a panel in class investigation. The major emphasis here is on learning about process rather than on learning about any particular topic, but we would hope that some content would be acquired.

Before students engage in this activity, the teacher might wish to review, in a formal discussion period, the types of questions in both domains, and the reasons for incorporating certain question types.

THE ACTIVITY. Basically the activity consists of allowing students to submit their questions to a panel of "judges" to determine if the questions are productive.

Students can alternate sitting on the "question" panel. Class members not on the panel are free to challenge the judgment of the panel, and by doing so they can gain valuable experience in "thinking through" their questions and the consequences of using particular questions. The entire activity can be scheduled before, during, or even after a specific lesson.

An information sheet can be provided for students or developed by them on which they record their questions and the panel's judgments. The format can resemble the following.

Questions for Panel Judgment

QUESTIONS	JUDGMENT AND REASON
1._____	_____
_____	_____
2._____	_____
_____	_____

My overall judgment regarding my questions

_____

_____

_____

This activity need not always involve a committee. Research teams consisting of two or three students can utilize this format to critique each other's questions before commencing an investigation.

Example. There is a science program which contains a unit entitled "Mystery Powders." The objective of the lesson is to allow students to employ numerous processes to discuss information and to formulate some conclusions regarding these powders. Assume that students are assigned this lesson, but before engaging in the lesson, they generate some questions deemed pertinent to the lesson's focus. An example of some probable questions follows.

Questions for Panel Judgment

TOPIC: Science, "Mystery Powders"

QUESTIONS	JUDGMENT AND REASON
How many powders are there?	Not really that good, for the number of powders will only tell you that, nothing more.
What is the color of the powders?	Ok, could give you a hint regarding what powders are.

Do the colors suggest what the powders are?	Ok, could lead you to a conclusion.
What will happen if I wet the powders?	Good, gets you thinking about how to process data.
Do the powders have any smell?	Good, may provide clue to powder identity.
Are there any powders that smell the same?	Good, gets you to compare.

My overall judgment of my questions. I asked pretty good questions, got me thinking about the powders and also ways to process the information.

Planning Activity 6: Determining the Function of Questions Planned

BASIC RATIONALE. In planning questions, students need to realize not only the cognitive level of their questions but also the purpose or function the questions serve. Will the questions raised stimulate divergent or convergent thinking and if so, is that the desired purpose? There are two guiding functions[1] that questions can serve: either centering or expansion. The centering function focuses a student's attention on a particular aspect of a topic under investigation; the expansion function focuses a student's attention on many possibilities or aspects of a topic being considered.

Students must understand that when they desire a few key ideas or conclusions their questions should serve a centering function, and when they wish numerous conclusions or myriad possible interpretations of particular data, their questions should serve an expansion function. Once they have determined the focus of their questions, learners need to ascertain if the questions are generating the desired function.

This particular activity stresses process rather than learning specific content, but of course once students have ascertained the functions of their questions, the activity can shift to using questions to gain understanding of specific or myriad topics.

Before students engage in this activity, they need a formal lesson or lessons on the functions of questions as they are incorporated into strategies.

THE ACTIVITY. The activity provides an opportunity for class members to record basic questions for investigation and to determine, either alone or with a fellow student, the questions' functions. The following format could be employed.

Question Function Check Sheet

SUBJECT AREA:_____

QUESTION	FUNCTION	
	CENTERING	EXPANSION
	(check appropriate space)	
1._____	_____	_____
	_____	_____
2._____	_____	_____
	_____	_____

Example. Suppose a teacher presents his class with a situation in which they are stranded in a wilderness area. He informs the class that they have a few things with them: a tea kettle, a role of plastic, a sheet of canvas, a flashlight, and some dried food. He identifies the object of the lesson as finding means of surviving in this setting and points out that the chance of survival depends largely upon the questions they raise and the answers obtained suggesting particular action. The teacher maintains that the focus will not be so much on the actual results, but rather on analyzing whether the questions raised were productive. Did their questions stimulate them to think of numerous ways to use the materials (expansion) or did the questions assist in focusing on a few optimal ways of using the materials (centering)?

Individual members of the group make a list of questions they wish to ask. The teacher reminds each of the students to contemplate why he or she is posing particular questions. Do I want to think of many things, and if so do my queries suggest that I consider things? Do I inquire what might happen if I change the use of some of the items? What would happen if I added to some of the items? What would happen if I subtracted from some of the items?

If I want to think of one or two uses for each item, do I ask questions that cause me to narrow down the material's uses, eliminating data not relevant? The teacher can assist learners in reacting by encouraging them to ask such questions.

Consider the sample lesson sheet that follows.

Question Function Check Sheet

SUBJECT AREA: Survival

QUESTIONS	FUNCTION	
	CENTERING	EXPANSION
What materials do I have with me?	*	
What is the major use of each good?	*	
What other way might I use the tea kettle?		*
Is there another way I can use the kettle besides that?		*
What would happen if I altered the shape of the tea kettle? Would it serve as a small stove?		*
What is the best use of this tea kettle?	*	
What are the properties of plastic?	*	
How can I take advantage of the properties of plastic?		*

Note. If a student experiences difficulty in determining whether her questions are serving an expansion or a centering function, ask her to pose this question: "Does the

question I have raised cause me to think of only a few
answers, or does the question I have posed cause me to think
of numerous answers?" By asking herself such questions as
she reviews the questions generated, she can determine their
function.

If the student really wished to think of many ways to
process some information or use some material, but most of
the questions she planned seemed to trigger thoughts about
only one or two things, then she has data informing her that
her questions are failing to do what she had intended them to
do.

Example. Today, with an increasing emphasis on
career education, educators at all levels of schools are striving
to incorporate the study of various jobs in the school curriculum. This expansion of the curriculum is causing content
and activities relating to industrial arts to find their way into
all levels and classes in the schools.

The Question Function Determination Activity can be
used in the areas of industrial arts in the following manner.

Assume that you are working with primary children and
wish them to handle simple tools like a hammer, saw, and
file. The lesson's objectives are to make a bird feeder and to
understand the use of these particular tools. Children need
to ask questions about when to use the hammer, when to
employ the saw, and when to use the file. Also, they need to
raise questions about what types and lengths of nails are required; about what types of materials—wood, glass, plastic—
they need; and how to put these materials together.

The children, at least some of them, are presented with
the job of making a bird feeder. The teacher can encourage
the children to raise some questions about the project. The
teacher informs the children they can ask some questions
which will help them think of one answer or they can raise
questions that will help them think of many answers. The
children can work individually or in groups.

The teacher can record on the chalkboard or on an over-
head transparency the children's questions to see if they

cause one to think of several things or only a few things. With this lesson focus, a question function check sheet such as the following might result. Notice that for this level, the title and divisions of the check sheet have been adjusted slightly.

Purposes of My Questions

SUBJECT: Building a bird feeder.
"Using new tools"

QUESTIONS	PURPOSES OF MY QUESTIONS	
	TO SUGGEST A FEW IDEAS	TO SUGGEST MANY IDEAS
Questions		
What do I have to do first?	*	
Why do we need a bird feeder?		*
What can I use to build one?		*
Which material will last the longest outdoors?	*	
What tools will I use to cut out the materials I select?	*	
What type of hammer do I need?	*	
How can I keep the bird feed dry?		*
How can I make birds notice the feeder?		*

Note. In the early elementary grades, children will need quite a bit of assistance in thinking of types of questions to ask. However, with experience in working with questions, children should become more independent.

Planning Activity 7: Question Flow Charts

BASIC RATIONALE. As previously mentioned, students need to realize possible directions for exploration by using specific types of questions and particular question sequences. Flow chart activity allows the learner to plan some major questions using a flow diagram and to indicate possible consequences of using such questions and then to generate additional questions along various paths. This activity is quite similar to developing reaction avenues except that the recording of the questions and responses differs.

This experience can relate to the open inductive discovery lesson, the structured inductive discovery lesson, as well as to the hypotheticodeductive discovery lesson, depending upon the teacher's objective. If students are to develop the flow charts for the purpose of discovery process only, it would qualify as the first type of discovery. If such planning is to facilitate student's discovering some information, then it would qualify as the structured inductive discovery lesson. However, if the first question is really a hypothesis to be tested, and the flow chart represents major questions posed for the testing, then the activity would qualify as hypotheticodeductive discovery.

THE ACTIVITY.   In this activity students record major questions and indicate plausible responses indicating pathways for additional questions. Class members can be introduced to the concept of feedback loop for referring back to previous or initial questions. Learners can then judge, either alone or with fellow classmates, if the planned flow has potential for assisting them in achieving the lesson's goal.

Example.   Contemplate learners in a social studies lesson confronting the question "What were some of the basic reasons for the Civil Rights Struggle?" Students ponder several questions and likely responses. The teacher informs class members to keep track of their questions and the directions their questions suggest by charting questions and answers in representative rectangles. An example of a student flow chart related to this focus might resemble the chart presented below.

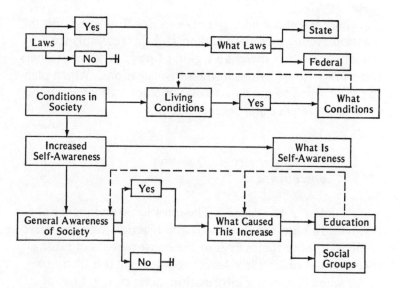

FIGURE 4-1 What Were Some Basic Reasons
for the Civil Rights Struggle?

Note. In the flow chart, students indicate choices
regarding directions in which to proceed and delineate some
major responses to particular questions. For instance, with
regard to the question of general awareness, once the student
had stated in the chart that "Yes, it was true that general
awareness had exerted some influence on civil rights activity," then he could raise the question "What caused this
increase?" In the example, the individual or individuals
posed two things that might have contributed to the increase. More possibilities could have been suggested.

How close this planned flow chart is to the actual execu-
tion of the lesson depends upon how meticulously the
students plan and also upon their prior level of knowledge. If
they knew little about the Civil Rights Struggle, they might
guess at what were some of the major reasons, but then they
would have to plan to investigate their hunches and their
flow charts would appear as a plan of "let's try these" directions.

There is some similarity between this flow chart and the reaction avenue presented earlier, and this resemblance demonstrates that there is a legion of ways in which learners can work with questions in their investigations. Which plan to use or when to use a particular one depends largely upon student preference and teacher's goal.

Planning Activity 8: Question Consequence

BASIC RATIONALE. The question consequence check is similar to both the flow chart and reaction avenues. Here students apprise themselves of the consequences of raising certain questions. It is valuable to know what is likely to occur when processing information along certain lines of questioning. Cognizance of the consequences enables students to ascertain if they really wish to employ particular questions or to generate new ones. It also clues learners to the types of materials needed, the environment required for the investigation, and the time needed for the inquiry.

This activity is designed to attune students to questions and to process. In one sense, it can be used to enable students to obtain insights into themselves. The types of questions they generate paint vivid self-portraits of their identity as students.

By centering on the consequences of questions, people become more careful planners of their investigations. Learners can achieve higher levels of questions and can anticipate future moves from consideration of their present questions.

THE ACTIVITY. The potential researchers delineate their desired questions and indicate in a parallel column results anticipated from utilization of such questions. The format is as follows:

Question Consequence Check

	QUESTION	CONSEQUENCE
1.	_____	_____
	_____	_____
2.	_____	_____
	_____	_____

My overall reaction

_____
_____
_____

In defending why their questions will have the consequences indicated, learners gain understanding of the types of information particular types of questions will procure. Again, the teacher can tie in the functions of questions to this consequence activity. Students will realize that if they wish to reach certain consequences, they will often need to adjust the function of their questions. This activity also can focus on the affective domain if the questions concern values, feelings, interests, and commitment to certain views. In such cases, the consequences not only might indicate situations, but also might identify necessary actions. For instance, if a person were studying health habits, and he posed a doubt regarding whether he valued the image of "the smoker," not only would the consequence provide some cognitive response such as "Yes, I do" or "No, I don't," but it also would suggest possible action for the questioner. If the student stated that he did not value the smoker image, but he was a smoker, then he has to ask himself if he will initiate an effort to alter his smoking behavior. If he does not, then this fact indicates that he does not value the nonsmoker image, at least not to the point of action

Example. Consider a science lesson dealing with ocean

exploration. Class members are encouraged to list questions they think important. The following check sheet might be produced by any member of the class.

Question Consequence Check

TOPIC: Ocean Exploration

QUESTIONS	CONSEQUENCES
Is there any going on today?	Will provide status information.
What is the purpose of the exploration?	Will provide a fact on purpose.
Who is involved?	Will provide names.
What areas of the ocean are being explored?	Identify facts of areas.
How deep is the ocean at the deepest point?	Provide specific facts.

My overall reaction:
    I don't like my questions too much as I look at them. They really don't tell me very much. Mostly, I have some facts, but I really am not getting at the reasons for the explorations or some of the benefits. I think I will think of some other questions.

Note. We might state that no student will engage in this self-criticism, and in the early stages of emphasizing questions in the class, this is probably so. However, learners will "measure up" if they are provided with opportunities to identify significant questions and to assess their consequences prior to using them. The teacher must schedule time for students to generate questions and to encourage learners to be critics of their own questions so that those posited will result in the production of meaningful data as well as additional questions.

*Planning Activity 9: Developing
Cognitive Maps*

BASIC RATIONALE. Students need to link their questions together in meaningful patterns to determine relationships among information they possess. Oftentimes students lack the means to organize their questions. The prime purpose of the cognitive map is similar to that of the reaction avenue in that it provides class members with a means for schematically indicating or mapping their inquiries or bits of data and relating major points to questions or information clusters.

THE ACTIVITY. The teacher has the students identify major questions and bits of information suggested by the queries. These are then mapped out, with horizontal lines indicating dimensions of data leading to higher order abstractions (see the sample following). After mapping their questions and major information points, students critique their maps to determine if the points emphasized and the questions generated will enable them to achieve their stated objective or objectives.

Example. Surmise that the teacher has introduced to his class a unit on the school. Community demands are being discussed, and the teacher posits "What will happen if alternative education becomes an integral part of the school?" The students are informed that they can consider the question from the positions of particular community groups involved or concerned with schooling: children, teachers, parents, administrators. The teacher has the class list these major populations as well as crucial data about the school. Before students commence their investigation they consider possible problem consequences that will affect the school in general and various community groups in particular. For this example, the teacher is interested in having his students identify consequences.

Cognitive Map

OBJECTIVE: To find as many possible responses to the question "What will happen if alternative education becomes an integral part of the school?"

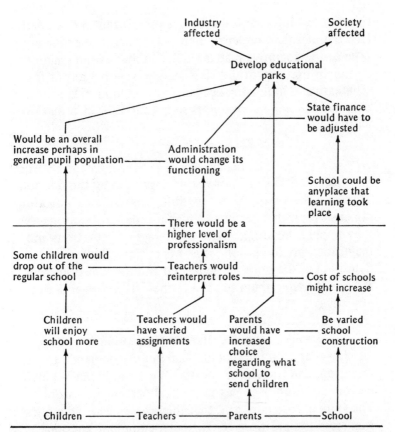

Taba developed the idea of a cognitive map. See *Teachers' Handbook for Elementary Social Studies* for details. (Reading, Massachusetts: Addison-Wesley, 1967). All the arrows lead to the tentative conclusion that educational parks would result. The map shows that investigation could branch out to consider how such parks would affect industry in society.

Note. The vertical lines describe avenues of investigation. The horizontal lines indicate increasing levels of complexity or abstraction. The questions are implied by the information bits. All the arrows lead to the tentative conclusion that educational parks would result. The map shows that investigations could branch out to consider how such parks would affect industry and society.

Planning Activity 10: Mapping Out Investigations; Special Emphasis on Particular Types of Questions

BASIC RATIONALE. This activity resembles the reaction avenue and cognitive map, but rather than identifying possible directions for investigation, it centers on the types of questions students can pose to process information at various stages of investigation. This activity emphasizes the affective as well as the cognitive domain in that the students are ascertaining their degree of satisfaction with specific types of questions and are evidencing a commitment to particular types of questions. Further, learners are revealing that they have conceptualized the value of good questioning by actually incorporating high-power questions into their investigatory procedures.

This activity requires students to have received formal lessons in question types and how to incorporate them in specific strategies. It assumes that students have discussed the steps required in processing information and have considered ways to create strategies aimed at discovering desired conclusions. This particular activity can set the stage for formal consideration of particular questioning strategies.

THE ACTIVITY. The teacher informs students that they are going to investigate a topic, selected by him, by them, or jointly selected. But before beginning they must carefully plan the necessary major steps of their investigation and possible questions for each step. Any one of several questioning or discovery strategies can be used, the important point being that students need to identify each step of the strategy and the particular questions they anticipate asking.

Example. Presume that students are to investigate the use of power in the community. With this focus, they might create a plan sheet such as the following:

Plan Sheet

Hunkins Combination Strategy*

TOPIC: The use of power in the community

STAGES OF THE STRATEGY	POSSIBLE TYPES OF QUESTIONS	QUESTIONS I WOULD ASK
Stage one	knowledge	What is the meaning of the term power?
	knowledge	What are some examples of power?
Stage two	comprehension	Explain what the author of my text said about power in the community.
Stage three	application	How can I obtain data to determine the power base in my community?
Stage four	analysis	Classify some of the results of particular demonstrations of power in my community.
		Indicate some of the basic assumptions of various power groups in my community.
Stage five	synthesis	What conclusion can I make about my community that might explain the power plays of another community?
Stage six	evaluation	Does my conclusion fit with the data I have gathered?

Reactions to my questions:
   My questions seem to be following the strategy.

*The Hunkins Combination Strategy is a procedure by which the teacher or students utilize questions at the various cognitive levels, usually working with

CONCLUDING NOTES

This chapter has presented several activities for engaging learners in planning or laying the foundation for planning effective questions for use in their investigations. These encounters were primarily concerned with having students comprehend process rather than specific content, but once students become skilled in using such planning techniques and obtain better insights into their questions, they can employ these activities as the initial step in their actual investigations in and outside of class.

The activities have not been sequenced by which should be done first, which second, and which last, for all are geared to the planning phase, either planning for the purpose of becoming more knowledgeable about questions or planning for the purpose of obtaining a clearer focus on some dimension of content.

Chapters 2 and 3 gave examples of questions in the cognitive and affective domains respectively. For the educator to assist learners in planning questions, he or she must know the several types of questions and means of planning questions. If the teacher has competence here, then he or she will assist students in becoming skilled in recognizing the various types of questions and more importantly, in being knowledgeable about when certain questions should be employed in active discovery.

No attempt was made to organize the activities closely by a particular mode of discovery. Nor was any effort made to organize activities by stressing of information processing, self-understanding, or behavior modification. The reader is free to make such organizations.

---

questions at the lower levels first and gradually phrasing questions at the upper cognitive levels. The questions have two purposes or functions: either to center the investigator's attention on specific data (centering) or to expand the investigator's attention to other cognitive levels; or to aim at uncovering greater depth at the same cognitive level (expansion).

A central aspect of the strategy is that as the individual is processing data at a particular cognitive level, he can pose questions which redirect his investigation to lower or higher cognitive levels when the need arises. For example, a person might be generating questions at the analysis level trying to identify key elements in a particular document. He is using questions with a centering function to arrive at one or two major issues. While using questions for this purpose and at this level, the investigator realizes that he needs some questions at the comprehension level to ascertain his basic understanding of the topic to which the document refers.

The strategy is termed Combination because it utilizes questions at the cognitive levels of Bloom's *Taxonomy* as well as combines the thinking of the author as to the manner in which one functions with these types of questions.

You can trust the student to engage in planning. The activities can contribute to an atmosphere where such planning can
occur so that the use of questions, as suggested in the next
chapter, will occur and be productive and enable the student to
be the major actor in the educational environment.

NOTES

1. FRANCIS P. HUNKINS, *Questioning Strategies and
Techniques* (Boston: Allyn and Bacon, Inc., 1972), pp. 81–88.

5

Involving Students in Using Questions and Questioning Strategies

INTRODUCTION

The second phase of working with questions is the actual use of questions in activities designed primarily for information gaining. In this phase, plans conceived in the planning stage are implemented.

The activities discussed in this chapter clearly relate to those suggested in the previous chapter in that the only reason for planning questions is to utilize them in some fashion. Therefore, even though these activities are presented in a separate chapter, in the actual school situation the teacher would have learners going through all three major stages: planning, implementing, and assessing.

This chapter is concerned with only the mid-stage of the central process system, the implementing or doing stage. The activities are not presented in a "do this first, this second" sequence. In-service and prospective teachers can decide which of these activities need to be done with their classes. Again, since learners may be working with these activities though the entire process loop—that is, going from planning, to implementing, to assessing activities—the students may decide the exact activities they wish to employ.

Many of these activities also provide opportunities in which the teacher can present formal lessons on questions and questioning in order to firm up the conceptual frameworks students have of questions. For example, activity 3, which centers on various questioning strategies, provides ample opportunities for students not only to perfect their questioning strategies, but to engage in investigating the dimensions of various strategies for the purpose of identifying common characteristics and synthesizing generalizations about strategies for processing information.

The encounters presented in this chapter have the same format as those in the previous chapter: basic rationale, the activity, an example, and related notes if pertinent. Most of the activities relate to modes of discovery for the purpose of gaining both an understanding of content and expertise in questioning behavior. The primary teaching model relates to that of the syntactical structure of the disciplines.

INVOLVEMENT ACTIVITIES

Involving Activity 1:
Role Playing Questions

BASIC RATIONALE. This exercise's prime purpose is to get students working with questions. Here individuals can formulate questions geared to a specific focus and can engage in a mini-investigation for one or two class periods, not so much to gain an understanding of the topic as to gain a command of using questions at various cognitive levels and in particular questioning sequences.

This activity could represent any of the various modes of discovery as suggested by Morine (see chapter 7), the exact mode depending upon the emphasis stressed by the teacher in structuring the lesson. Most likely, it would be good for students to experience all of these modes of discovery and to determine for themselves their questioning facility when functioning in different modes. Of course, the teacher must keep in mind the age level of the learner when deciding which mode is to be stressed.

THE ACTIVITY. This role playing would follow from one or more of the previous planning activities. Here the teacher provides the class with a focus, a problem in an inductive lesson, a hypothesis in a deductive discovery lesson. Of course, the students, at times, can suggest their own focus. The teacher informs the class that they will have one or two periods to process the data by raising questions and obtaining answers to their questions. Materials are provided for this mini-investigation. Data resulting from posing the questions are recorded on some type of data chart and the teacher points out to the class that they can refer to previous notes regarding how to process information and plan their questions.

Students can be organized into teams for this mini-investigation. Often, such organization will facilitate question generation and provide a forum in which learners can discuss their findings before reporting their conclusions to the total class.

Example. The teacher presents the following problem to a science class. A farmer in a particular state discovers that part of his corn crop is either dying or not growing to optimal height. Desiring to correct the situation, he calls in a team from the university to consider his plight and to suggest a solution. The students role-play the scientists.

Class members working in the teams might begin by posing questions relating to the location of the problem, whether the problem had occurred previously. The teams should ask questions to lay a data foundation and record the resulting facts on a chart. (Note: The teacher has supplied materials and primary sources for student use.) The students may record questions on a reaction avenue. The central question is "Why is the corn not growing as well as it should?" A student team could list possible reasons: lack of water, poor quality seed, lack of fertilizer, insufficient sunshine. Questions to ascertain just factual information may be asked. Once a data base has been developed, investigators might pose questions comparing this farmer's corn crop with crops of other farmers in the area. Students might focus on the location of this crop to other crops of corn. "What is different; the same?" "Is there anything that occurs near this crop that does not occur with other corn crops?" Questions at the analysis level, used to identify significant elements and to analyze relationships among these elements, might be asked at this stage. Students record the information uncovered.

At the end of the mini-session, students indicate tentative conclusions regarding this problem and their suggested solution or solutions. The teacher then schedules time for comparison of results, a debriefing session. This time student investigators listen to each others' judgments and rank the conclusions advanced. Learners discuss their questions and indicate the rationales for them. From such discussions, learners not only firm up their understanding of the topic, but also gain needed experience in the process.

Note. A productive practice is to have one member of each team serve as a recorder of the questions being raised and responded to in this mini-investigation. This practice provides material on questions that can be used later in self-analysis and future planning of similar investigations.

*Involving Activity 2: Resource
Person Visit*

BASIC RATIONALE. Frequently people visit the
school to provide information and insights relating to particular topics that cannot be gained from class study. Often
classes use resource persons inefficiently due to poorly
planned questions. The result is an experience focusing on
specifics or issues which could easily be answered in class
material rather than focusing on issues and concerns that best
use the talents of the visiting individual.

It is crucial for students to take time prior to the visitor's
arrival to consider what questions they wish to pose and to
determine if this expert can provide insights not available in
other materials or via other means.

THE ACTIVITY. The activity has two basic stages: the
planning stage and the doing stage. It is during the planning
stage that key questions are determined and sequenced.
When the questions are presented in a meaningful sequence,
the resource person is assisted in developing a productive
discussion. It might be helpful to provide this consultant
with the list of questions before he arrives to assist him in
organizing his presentation.

The doing stage commences when the speaker arrives. As
he discusses his topic, students, using a check sheet, indicate
those questions being answered and make some abbreviated
notations. Then when he begins his conclusion and/or asks
for questions, the students can quickly skim over their lists
and determine unanswered questions needing elaboration.
Such a listing and checking off of questions also allows students some basis for challenging, of course in a friendly way,
the views of the visitor or his interpretations of the topic
under consideration.

Example. Contemplate students in a creative writing
class who have arranged a visit by a local writer to discuss her

works. In the planning stage, the students have identified some major questions they wish to ask and organized them into a sequence. The questions are recorded on a sheet such as the following.

Resource Person Visit

TOPIC: Creative writing

MAJOR QUESTIONS

We would like to know some of your thinking that caused you to write your latest work.

What is the main reason for the story?

If we interpret the actions of the main character in this way, would you agree with that interpretation?

A most significant event in the story is when the man decides to stay with the job out of obligation to his family. Do you think that is a realistic aspect of the plot in light of today's society?

How did you manage to keep the excitement of the story right up to the last page? What are some techniques that a writer employs to maintain reader tension?

Students can test these questions out with their classmates to see if they are worthwhile and to determine if they are placed in a meaningful sequence. This list can be sent to the resource person. Upon the writer's arrival, one or two students can sit with the writer and pose questions to which the writer is to respond. Students in their seats can jot down the responses and also note other inquiries suggested.

This activity serves the dual purpose of providing students with practice in creating questions for interviews as well as employing questions to learn something about the purposes and techniques of writers.

*Involving Activity 3: Using Various
Questioning Strategies*

BASIC RATIONALE.   The central purpose for stressing questions is to provide learners with requisite skills for using questions in various strategies. These strategies can follow numerous models as suggested in several sources mentioned previously. This activity, which can be repeated each time the teacher uses a different strategy, is based on the assumption that the only way learners become skilled questioners and critical inquirers is through having opportunities to raise and use questions and to challenge information encountered in school as well as outside of school.

Which mode of discovery the students avail themselves of is not important provided they realize which one they are using and are cognizant of the reasons for their particular tack. Activity 3 provides students with experiences in all modes of discovery (see chapter 7 for details on these modes) as well as immersion in work with various models of teaching, in this case self-teaching.

In essence, this activity can provide students with opportunities to practice particular strategies encountered in more formal teaching situations. If students are to apply particular strategies when processing information, then lessons in the basic aspects of each of these strategies must be provided. A strategy could be identified, discussed, and activity 3 could be used when a particular topic is under investigation. Then assessing sessions could be held under the direction of the teacher in which students compared their use of the strategy with the model of the strategy presented formally.

This activity does assume that students have had some instruction in means of identifying particular strategies. Perhaps, in some structured lesson, the teacher has had students make a checksheet for monitoring certain strategies to determine if specific strategy components are being used. The strategy-use monitoring sheet provides one means by which students can identify particular strategies.

Not all formal lessons on the strategies have to be expository. Indeed, they should not be so. Formal situations can be designed in which students encounter an individual in a particular situation employing a certain strategy. With the teacher's guidance, students can inquire about the type of strategy the person was using, the specific types of questions employed, and the major thrust of the strategy. Such "formal" discovery sessions on strategy use give students skill in putting to use their understanding of questions. This use of information certainly provides students with an increased conceptual understanding of questions and related strategies.

THE ACTIVITY. This is really not just one activity, but rather a basic grouping of activities in which learners apply particular questioning strategies to specific topics. For an example, let us assume that students have just learned the Hunkins Combination Strategy.[1] This strategy employs questions utilizing the question classification scheme set forth in Bloom's *Taxonomy.* Basically, a person utilizing the strategy develops questions at various cognitive levels, usually commencing with questions at the lower levels and progressively working with increasingly higher level questions as the inquiry continues. The questions are formulated to direct the investigator to engage in either convergent or divergent thinking. Occasionally, the inquirer would have to redirect his or her questions to lower cognitive levels to obtain background information necessary for the continuation of the search. The prime objective of the strategy is to have the student process information at various cognitive levels via questioning, with the result being a conclusion in the form of a concept, generalization, law, or understanding. The final step of the strategy enables the individual to utilize evaluation questions to determine if his or her conclusion is valid or warranted based on the data processed at the previous stages in the strategy.

In this activity, learners are given time to apply the strategies to a topic. The application of the strategy would involve some of the planning activities previously mentioned, as well as some of the diagnostic activities yet to be discussed.

If a teacher wished her students to become adept at employing five strategies, she would provide at least five activities in which students would function with a particular strategy. Of course, the use of any one strategy could take from one to several days, perhaps even weeks. Students functioning in a process-oriented curriculum would be in activities in which they actually employed scientific questioning strategies in situations both within and outside the school.

The teacher can employ several types of formats with this activity. The important point is to provide students with some means of identifying the strategy they are employing, the reason or reasons for their use of the strategy, the topic investigated with the strategy, and some means of deciding and assessing their reactions to the strategy used.

One possible form is provided below.

Sample Strategy Use Monitoring Sheet

Subject Area _____

Central topic: _____

Strategy selected _____
_____

Reason for strategy selection: _____
_____

Key question/s to initiate the use of the strategy: _____
_____
_____
_____

General perceptions regarding strategy use: _____
_____
_____

Type of information, conclusions derived with strategy: _____
_____
_____
_____
_____
_____

My judgment regarding my use of strategy: _____

_____

_____

_____

Good points: _____

Points needing improvement: _____

Overall reaction to my use of strategy with this lesson focus: _____

_____

_____

Educators need to provide adequate time for students to utilize several questioning strategies. Not only does processing knowledge via these strategies consume time, but planning the strategy as well as diagnosing the effectiveness of the questioner's deployment of strategies necessitates additional time and comprises a crucial dimension of the total learning process. Education using process strategies is slower than education employing a dominant use of expository methods, but education should be concerned with having students engaged in their learning, and not just responding to information presented to them.

Example. Many school districts have trouble passing special levies for the support of the school. Consider a class in a district with this problem. The teacher informs the class that individuals interested in investigating why the community is having difficulty in passing levies can do so. The teacher asks students to use the Strategy Use Monitoring Sheet to record information for a later debriefing session.

Following is an example of what one student's sheet might look like.

Strategy Use Monitoring Sheet
_____

SUBJECT AREA: Sociology
CENTRAL TOPIC: Failures of school special levies

STRATEGY SELECTED: Hunkins Combination Strategy

REASON FOR STRATEGY SELECTION: This strategy will allow me to process information at higher cognitive levels and enable me to arrive at some type of conclusion.

KEY QUESTIONS TO INITIATE THE USE OF THE STRATEGY: "What are some major reasons for the failure of my community's school levies?"

GENERAL PERCEPTIONS REGARDING STRATEGY USE: I began the investigation by using questions at the knowledge level and tried using these questions in such a way as to help me think of as many reasons for the failure as possible. I followed some of the question leads and checked community newspapers for the reprints and editorials on the issue. I used analysis questions to get at some of the major arguments.

TYPE OF INFORMATION, CONCLUSION DERIVED WITH THIS STRATEGY: I used analysis questions to identify some major arguments of prominent community members. My questions helped me to see how the views of these people influenced others in the community.

I discovered that the major concern was with the rise in local taxes and the fact that one area of the curriculum was considered controversial by some.

MY JUDGMENT REGARDING MY USE OF THE STRATEGY: I think I used the strategy fairly well, for I did get some information that I had not thought of before.

GOOD POINTS: I asked questions at the upper cognitive levels.

POINTS NEEDING IMPROVEMENT: I could have asked more high-level questions. I often did not redirect my questions to lower levels when needed. I think I was satisfied with the first answer I found. I did not use the questions to expand my thinking as much as I could have.

OVERALL REACTION: I think I can use the strategy fairly well. I like the idea of being able to ask my own questions and investigate what I think is important.

Example. This second example points out that questioning strategies can be utilized in many "hands on" types of activities. Assume you are teaching a class in metal working at the secondary level. Your lesson's purpose is to assist students in planning questions to comprise a strategy for studying the techniques of working with particular metals. Specifically, the lesson's focus is on metal forming using bending machines. From such a lesson, the following sheet might be produced by a student.

Specific Strategy Use Monitoring Sheet

SUBJECT AREA: Metal working

GENERAL TOPIC: Procedures for metal forming

GENERAL OBJECTIVE: To make a portable workbench from aluminum and related alloys.

STRATEGY SELECTED: Hunkins Combination Strategy

REASON FOR STRATEGY SELECTION: This strategy will allow me to raise questions about the key characteristics of certain metals. Also this strategy will help me to learn about the characteristics of these metals that I need to remember when using the bending machine.

KEY QUESTIONS TO INITIATE THE USE OF THE STRATEGY: Which form or forms do I need to finish my metal portable work bench?

Which metals have both strength and lightness?

TYPE OF INFORMATION, CONCLUSIONS DERIVED WITH THE STRATEGY: I started out with knowledge questions to determine the forms needed and metals with the characteristics of lightness and strength. Before I made the final selection of the metal, I asked myself some understanding (comprehension) questions relating to tensile strength of several metals I had. I also raised questions about the cost of materials.

I posed questions to find out how much pressure my bending machine could exert.

As I engaged in the bending process, I would stop the process every so often and check the metal being formed. At these times, I raised questions that forced me to check the surface of the metal for any resulting defects. I also asked myself some questions which forced me to compare the resulting form with my drawing of the form I desired.

Toward the end of the bending process, I asked questions that helped me consider whether I had made the best choice of material for my task.

I asked questions that helped me find out how this metal reacted in this stress situation. I reached some conclusions about the tensile strength and flexibility of the metal.

MY JUDGMENT REGARDING MY USE OF THE STRATEGY: I think I did a good job with the strategy. I used questions throughout the bending process to check my actions.

POINTS NEEDING IMPROVEMENT: I may have spent too much time asking questions just dealing with facts. I really knew this information. I need to ask questions dealing more specifically with how the metal responds to differing pressures.

OVERALL REACTION: I enjoyed using the strategy. Before I learned it, I usually just did something in metal class and did not ask any questions except "How does it look" after using the bending machine. I think I know more about metals now.

Note. The important point to remember regarding this activity is that students need to be involved in questioning and require some means of monitoring or recording their involvement. By keeping a record of their strategies, students can gain a greater understanding of the technique in use and also can begin to see which strategies are productive in particular situations. Furthermore, by such activities, students realize that questions are integral parts of all strategies and greatly influence the quality of the information obtained from the school experience. The learning is twofold; students are learning about the topic, in this case metal working, but they also are learning about questioning strategies. Both are crucial domains of knowledge.

Involving Activity 4: Analyzing Questions in Materials

BASIC RATIONALE. Besides having awareness of and skill in generating questions for their inquiries, students should consider the questions contained in materials they encounter both in and out of school. Oftentimes, learners assume that questions incorporated in written materials have high cognitive levels. Upon analysis, they are surprised to discover that many materials, textbooks, and trade books use few questions and those that do often utilize inquiries stressing knowledge and comprehension levels. From such analysis, class members can discern the quality of the questions in materials they use and can determine if they need to upgrade the questions in their materials for a closer cognitive or affective fit with the questions they are generating in particular strategies.

THE ACTIVITY. The teacher has learners analyze questions in the legions of materials present in and out of school. Students record on a form the types of questions encountered, and indicate their judgments of worth. Oftentimes, students can take these recorded questions and rephrase them into high-order questions more suitable to a particular class investigation.

The form might resemble the following one.

Questions in Materials

SOURCE ANALYZED: _____

PAGES ANALYZED: _____

SUBJECT AREA OF SOURCE: _____

QUESTIONS LISTED	PAGES	COGNITIVE/ AFFECTIVE LEVEL
1. _____		_____
_____	____	_____
2. _____	____	_____
3. _____	____	_____
_____	____	_____

General Reactions to questions present in this material: _____

_____

_____

Example. Contemplate a class studying communism and reading an article written by Barbara Ward.[2] The class has already read the article, but now the teacher urges the students to reread and analyze the questions used by the author. For the sake of the example learners consider the following portion of the article.

What are these presuppositions? Perhaps before I outline them, I should allow for one possibility. Are we conceivably living in the final decades of pure communist orthodoxy? The appearance of Titoism on the world stage and all the current discussions of "different roads to Socialism" may presage the beginnings of a whole spectrum of communist faiths, allied yet different, as are the sects of Christianity. We can still talk of communist orthodoxy today. But in twenty years time, shall we be able to say so emphatically what communism is?[3]

Questions in Materials

SOURCE ANALYZED: *Five Ideas That Change the World*, Barbara
                 Ward
SUBJECT AREA OF SOURCE: Social studies, communism.
PAGES ANALYZED:

QUESTIONS LISTED	PAGES	COGNITIVE/ AFFECTIVE LEVEL	
What are these presuppositions?	_____	Comp.	Resp.
Are we conceivably living in the final decades of pure communist orthodoxy?	_____	Comp.	Resp.
But in twenty years time shall we be able to say emphatically what communism is?	_____	Analysis	

From such a list the student can discern that two questions are at the comprehension level and that two of them have the affective level of responding or getting the individual to respond to the issue of communism. The third question might well be analysis centering on recognizing basic assumptions.

This activity allows students to determine the level of the questions in the materials with which they will be dealing to see if they need to adjust their aims and to adjust the questions in the materials to agree more closely with their objectives. The skills that learners have acquired in other class sessions in formulating and recognizing questions at various cognitive and affective levels can be utilized at this juncture. Additionally, such an activity makes students aware of the questions that exist in the materials they read and also to realize that oftentimes the materials they encounter do not have any questions.

Involving Activity 5: Question Games

BASIC RATIONALE. Question games is really a type of activity rather than a specific one. Here attention is on creating encounters to allow students to develop skill in formulating questions and/or recognizing types of questions. A good reference is Gillin et al., *Questioneze*,[4] which lists possible games that can be played to increase student's skill in question recognition and formulation. But the teacher does not always have to go by a book; he or she can motivate students to create their own games for improving their questions and questioning skill.

In reality, Involving Activity 5 is a formal lesson on question types, for the teacher often can provide particular examples of questions at specific levels prior to the game. The resultant discussions also clarify for students their understanding of specific types of questions in the cognitive and affective domains.

ACTIVITY A. One type of activity presents students with a slide of some particular situation, event, or person and gives them three minutes to come up with questions at a particular cognitive or affective level. The level can be determined by picking a slip of paper out of a hat with a number representing a cognitive or affective level. For example, number four might represent analysis at the cognitive level. The teacher draws a four and students write as many analysis questions as possible relating to the slide focus. A form similar to the following can be employed.

Question Game—Write the Question

FOCUS: _____

Questions (level determined by the number drawn from hat)

1. _____
2. _____
3. _____
4. _____
5. _____
6. _____

Assessment of questions produced: _____

Note. Schedule time for class members to share their questions and to judge whether they are really at the appropriate level. The game also can be played with the numbers referring to questions in the affective domain.

ACTIVITY B. Another game that can be played is to present a problem situation and then have students generate question types that can assist in achieving the needed conclusion. The teacher can have the situations presented on cards or they can be recorded on cassette tapes. Students can work in teams. The following form might be used.

Question for the Situation

SITUATION: (verbal or audio)

Questions needed for achievement of objective:

_____
_____
_____
_____
_____

Question critique: _____

Note. The question critique in this game allows class-mates to discuss whether they asked optimal questions for obtaining the type of conclusions suggested in the situation. The idea of gaming or simulations continues to gain popularity. These particular games center primarily on students recognizing and producing questions at particular cognitive or affective levels. When one wishes individuals to organize questions into questioning strategies, some of the mini-investigations or role-playing activities discussed previously might be useful.

Example for Activity B. A class working in plane geometry is given the following problem to prove: the bisectors of the base angles of an isosceles triangle form with the base another isosceles triangle. The situation in this case is written on the chalk board as follows:

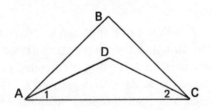

FIGURE 5-1   Isosceles Triangle.

Questions for Situation

Questions needed for achievement of objective:
What is the definition of an isosceles triangle?
Identify the givens in the situation.
Judge whether all the givens are relevant to the problem.
Determine what AD does to angle ABC.
What does CD do to angle BCA?
What do I recall about the method of proof?
What are the characteristics of such triangles?

Question Critique: My questions centered on knowledge, analysis, evaluation, comprehension, and knowledge again. But I needed to ask some questions about how to go about proving the problem suggested in the original question.

Example to Activity A. Following is an example taken from *Questioneze*[5] by Gillin et al. This game is to be played with groups of students numbering from three to six. The game's objective is to determine if students can create questions at various cognitive levels in response to specific pictures presented for focus. It could also be used for giving students practice in writing questions at affective levels.

There are two possible roles: the role of player and that of judge. According to the rules, the judge is appointed first by the coordinator who is the teacher. After the first round of the game, this role is rotated around the group.

The game's rules indicate that the judge is to select a picture from the *Questioneze* manual and students are to generate questions about it, the level of the question being determined by the throw of a die. If the die reads one, then the questions are to be at the knowledge level (receiving, if the affective domain), while if the die reads two, the questions are to be at the comprehension level, and so forth.

Players have two minutes to formulate their questions after which time they read them aloud and the judge determines if the questions are at the intended level. Players may challenge the judge's decision. Other players can vote if there is disagreement between the judge and the person who formed the question. Players receive a number of points, to be determined by the teacher or by the players, for each question judged appropriate for an indicated level. The points are tallied after all students have had a turn.

Suppose the student judge selects the picture in Figure 5-2.

The judge casts the die, and it reads four. Students are given two minutes to write an analysis question. After two

FIGURE 5-2   "Questioneze" illustration.

Caroline J. Gillin et al., *Questioneze* (Columbus, Ohio: Charles E. Merrill, 1972), p. 37.

minutes, the first student suggests the following question, "Categorize the major elements of this picture that carry a message." The judge decides that the question is on target. A second student volunteers his question, "What is the meaning of the circles at the top of the page?" The judge votes that this is not an analysis question but a comprehension question related to understanding the use of symbols. The rest of the student group supports his judgment. The game continues until all students have provided questions at the analysis level. The judge's role then shifts to the next student in line and the die is tossed again. This time it shows a six, meaning that evaluation questions should be written. The procedure is repeated until students have written questions at all levels.

Suppose the game shifted to creating affective level questions. (Note: *Questioneze* does not consider affective questions.) The die is thrown and it reads three, valuing. One student might pose the following question, "Would you be interested in living in the type of environment suggested in the drawing?" The judge ranks the question as being appropriate. Student two asks the following, "Would I prefer to live in this environment over the one in which I currently live? The judge ranks that question as on target.

Note. This type of game, done with photographs or slides as well, gives students practice in creating questions at several levels of both domains and provides learners with experience in defending their questions. Further, it enables individuals, when playing the role of judge, to protect their skills in assessing the levels of questions. How long students play this game depends upon their age level and how much practice they need in formulating questions at particular levels.

A variation of this activity might have students asking questions at a particular level each day about a specific event displayed in a class interest center. For instance, on Monday, questions at the knowledge level could be raised and recorded; on Tuesday, comprehension questions could be advanced about the focus. At the end of the week, the class can review and evaluate the questions raised. Such an activity helps students realize that questions at a multitude of levels can be posed regarding the same focus.

Another type of game is to provide a picture focus and to ask students, alone or in groups, to formulate questions at each cognitive or affective level relating to the same focus. For example, if learners were shown a picture of wheat growing, they might generate the following questions.

>   (Knowledge) What is wheat?
>
>   (Comprehension) What do I understand about how wheat is grown?
>
>   (Application) If wheat is growing poorly, which of the following reasons would account for it?
>
>   (Analysis) Indicate the relationship among wheat, climate, and soil conditions suggested in this picture.
>
>   (Synthesis) Create a statement about how man uses wheat.
>
>   (Evaluation) Is our use of wheat the best we can make of this crop?

*Involving Activity 6: Matching
Questions with Materials*

BASIC RATIONALE.   Learners need to realize that different types of materials can trigger several types of questions. For example, books which are very explicit have a tendency to use and foster the formation of knowledge and comprehension questions. Primary source materials, like letters, legal documents, charts, mathematical formulae, or photographs, tend to encourage students to pose questions at higher cognitive levels. There is not a firm rule that states this always will be the case, but it does occur often enough to qualify as a useful rule of thumb for the teacher or teacher-to-be.

THE ACTIVITY. The teacher or some appointed student collects several types of materials in the classroom. These materials may comprise an interest center relating to some content area of the curriculum. Students can group materials by type and then record the varieties of questions they discover in these materials. If no questions exist to indicate the types of questions that come to mind when reading the material, the students can work in teams of two and discuss their reactions. The data and attendant perceptions are recorded on a form similar to the one which follows for classroom sharing.

Materials—Questions Match

CONTENT AREA/S: _____

MATERIALS (TYPE)	QUESTIONS (TYPE) (PRESENT OR SUGGESTED)
letter	analysis questions
legal document	comprehension, analysis
chart	questions

Conclusions about questions and material types: _____

Example. In this example students are given a portion of The Mayflower Compact to read and to determine the questions present or implied by the document.

The Mayflower Compact 1620

In the name of God, Amen. We ... the Loyal Subjects of our dread Soverign Lord King James, by the Grace of God, of Great Britain, France, and Ireland, King Defender of the Fair. Having undertaken the Glory of God, and the Advancement of the Christian Faith and the Honor of our King and Country, a Voyage to plant the first colony in the northern parts of Virginia do by these Presents solemnly and mutually in the Presence of God and one another, covenant and combine ourselves together into a civil Body Politic, for our better Ordering and Preservation, and Furtherance of the Ends aforesaid: and by Virtue hereof Laws, Ordinances, Acts, Constitutions, and Offices from time to time, as shall be thought most meet and convenient for the general Good of the Colony: until which we promise all due Submission and Obedience.[6]

Materials—Questions Match

CONTENT AREA: Social Studies

MATERIALS (Type)	QUESTION (Type)
Document, Mayflower Compact	No question in document, but it does suggest the following:
	What was the central thrust of the document?
	What was the reason for the document?
	Indicate the powers of the King.
	Identify who these people were.
	Categorize the powers of the King.
	Distinguish the central assumptions regarding the views of these people toward their world.

Conclusions about questions: This document allows the reader, really makes him or her, to ask questions at the higher levels. If I only ask questions dealing with facts, I do not get too much information from the document.

Note. It is important that the teacher schedules time for sharing perceptions resulting from the materials and question analysis. Such sharing enables persons to utilize additional questions in improving their knowledge of process, in this case questioning. Such knowledge is most useful for it cuts across all subject areas. It can be considered as instrumental process rather than content specific process. Through such an activity students also can learn about the several types of process available for their use.

Example. Matching questions with materials can be used in all areas of the curriculum. A teacher in home economics can employ the activity to have students gain expertise in raising questions at several cognitive and affective levels. Let us assume that a teacher is working with early high school students in a home economics class dealing with planning variety in meals without sacrificing nutritional value. Students have studied nutrition and have some knowledge of the chemistry of digestion. The teacher has brought into class books on planning meals and pamphlets dealing with the psychological aspects of variety in meals.

With this background, the teacher guides students, working in teams of two, to react to the types of materials they have covered in class focusing on the questions stated or implied. The following materials—question match form might be generated by one student team.

Materials—Question Match

CONTENT AREA: Home economics, meal variety

MATERIALS (Types)	QUESTIONS (Types)
Books on nutrition, meal planning, menu variety	Indicate some major reasons for meal planning. (Knowledge)
Pamphlets on digestion chemistry	List the types of food you would eat willingly. (Responding)
	Discuss the essential elements needed to trigger digestion. (Knowledge-Comprehension)
Pamphlet on psychological aspect of meal variety.	Explain in your own words how variety affects peoples' eating habits. (Comprehension)
	What is a basic assumption regarding the use of organic foods? (Analysis)

Conclusions about questions: These materials have questions that can get a student to function at some of the higher cognitive levels. Also, some of the materials have questions which focus on values and beliefs regarding food use and nutrition.

Note. The questions in this match represent only a sampling. Certainly, students dealing with this subject area would discover many types of questions. As students become more experienced in dealing with questions, they may take some of the types of questions they discover and rephrase them in order to increase their cognitive and affective levels. Of course, the exercise as presented assumes that students have had some formal training in types of questions. Therefore, the activity provides students with an opportunity to apply their understandings of questions.

Involving Activity 7:
Extrapolating Questions

BASIC RATIONALE. Students need to develop their creative powers in generating questions for guiding their learning. This activity, somewhat similar to the previous one, is designed to stimulate the creative thinking of students with regard to questions. The activity relates to the discovery of process but locates more precisely within the open inductive discovery mode, for the individual is not dealing with a specific question, but seeks to discover as many questions as possible that are pertinent to the focus provided. This situation assumes that students, encouraged to develop questions, will attain higher levels of thinking and develop a higher level of commitment to being active learners.

THE ACTIVITY. The teacher provides the class with several types of materials and asks the students to think of as many questions as possible at as many levels in both the cognitive and affective domains as they can. They are to list these questions on the sheet provided. After this session, a class debriefing can be held in which learners react to their questions and challenge classmates about whether their questions are at the levels claimed.

This is similar to the brainstorming activity indicated previously, but it differs in that it relates to specific types of materials and is within the materials phase of class investigations.

A form similar to the one below can be used by students to record their questions.

Extrapolating Questions
_____

MATERIAL 1 ENCOUNTERED: _____
Questions suggested:

_____

_____

_____

_____

MATERIAL 2 ENCOUNTERED: _____
Questions suggested:

_____

_____

MATERIAL 3 ENCOUNTERED: _____
Questions suggested:

_____

_____

_____

General conclusions/reactions: _____

_____

_____

_____

Example. A class is involved in studying the methods by which people express their feelings: poems, essays, short stories, novels. For purposes of comparison the teacher has his class consider the emotion of love for one's fellow human beings and he has brought to class examples of several forms of writing dealing with this topic. A resulting extrapolation chart might resemble the following.

Extrapolating Questions

MATERIAL 1 ENCOUNTERED: Poem
Questions suggested:
>   What type of poem?
>   Do I agree with the poem's message?
>   Have I ever thought about this topic before?
>   How would I rephrase the poem?

MATERIAL 2 ENCOUNTERED: Essay
Questions suggested:
>   Give an example of the type of situation the person is referring to.
>   Can I tell the essay in my own words?
>   What conclusion can I deduce from this essay?
>   Have I ever behaved in the way described in the essay?

General Conclusions: Reactions-
>   My questions are at several cognitive and affective levels. I like my questions for they get me thinking.

Learners should practice generating questions as they react to class materials and should record their questions for later analysis and sharing with class colleagues. In this manner they increase their knowledge of questions and also achieve a deeper understanding of the materials considered.

Involving Activity 8: Developing Novel Use of Questions

BASIC RATIONALE.   Learners require opportunities to create uncommon uses for questions with regard to common materials. For example, students view films and filmstrips quite often and usually respond to questions about what the film reported or what they saw, and such questions are fine, but they only exist at the knowledge or comprehension levels. Also, such questions usually do not emphasize the affective domain. Learners need situations in which they employ materials and media in ways which stimulate effective questions in both domains. Again, this activity closely resembles the previous activity since it is using materials to trigger students' questioning.

THE ACTIVITY. Have students view a film or filmstrip several times. Each time have the class view only a portion of the film. On the first viewing, class members list all the knowledge questions they would like to ask. On the second viewing, they delineate comprehension questions deemed important. On a third showing, have the students include analysis questions they consider vital to their investigation. You can then engage the class in a discussion relating to how their perceptions changed in viewing the film when they centered on questions at different cognitive levels. Their questions and reactions can be recorded on a form which could be included in a notebook.

Novel Use of Questions

FILMSTRIP — First viewing (knowledge questions suggested)
Questions: _____

_____

_____

FILMSTRIP — Second viewing (comprehension questions suggested)
Questions: _____

_____

_____

FILMSTRIP — Third viewing (analysis questions suggested)
Questions: _____

_____

_____

Another variation is to have students view the middle portions of films or filmstrips and to suggest questions designed to formulate conclusions. After this has been done, the end of the film could be viewed and students could ascertain if the questions enabled them to reach a conclusion similar to the one advanced in the film.

Note. Under novel use of questions, time could be provided for students to brainstorm diverse ways in which questions can be used. Learners can discover that questions can be used to initiate discussion or to close discussion if the dialogue was leading to erroneous conclusions. Questions can be used for dealing with individuals in particular ways. For instance, students can discover that if some of them have little concern for others, the careful use of questions, especially in the affective domain, can cause individuals to stop and access just how they are relating to others.

Example. As part of the Suchman inquiry science materials produced by SRA, there were several film loops that revealed particular situations which individuals were to inquire about. Assume that a teacher has one of the film-loops that shows a small model sailboat in a tub of water. A person holds a fan in his hand and directs the flow of air at the sail, and the boat moves. The next portion of the film loop shows the fan placed on the boat. When the fan is turned on with the flow of air directed at the sail, the boat does not move. The major question is, why does the boat move the first time and not the second?

On the first consideration of the filmloop, have the students list knowledge questions that come to mind. On the second viewing, have students record questions at the comprehensive level. This can be considered until questions at each level are advanced. Of course, some levels of questions may be skipped. Students record these on a sheet and then use them to gain data from the teacher. This particular example uses a model of inquiry which is quite specific and follows very closely particular ground rules.[7]

Using this example, a question chart such as the following can be made.

Use of Questions

TOPIC: Science, Focus, Sailboat
FILMLOOP: First Viewing (Knowledge Questions)
Questions:
  How big was the boat?
  What was the boat placed in?
  What was the shape of the boat?
  How low did the boat sink in the liquid?
  Where was the fan placed the first time?
  Where was the fan placed the second time?
  Was the speed of the fan the same both times?
  Was the boat touching the side of the container?
  Did the liquid have the color of water?
FILMLOOP: Second Viewing (Comprehension Questions)
  What were the differences about the placement of the fan the
      first and second time?
  What might happen if the fan were on the boat but not blowing
      into the sail?
  What do I know about the relation of the speed of the fan to the
      force of wind current generated?
  Is there more resistance to a boat low down in the water than to
      one riding high on the surface?
FILMLOOP: Third Viewing (Analysis Questions, Application
              Questions)
  What can I do to make the boat move again?
  Which of the following rules regarding motion and force might
      offer some explanation?
  What hypothesis could I phrase from analysis of this phenomena?
  What are the crucial factors in the example that relate to the use of
      force and movement?
  What are the groupings of actions and reactions in the example that
      would enable the boat to move, that would prevent movement
      of the boat?

After this activity, the students can actually engage in inquiry. This is really a preliminary step that allows the students to do some thinking before becoming involved. Hopefully such "before" action will improve the quality of questions asked.

Involving Activity 9:
Questions Trial

BASIC RATIONALE. Often, students are so involved in investigating topics as part of their studies that they do not take the time to try out their questions before beginning the major investigation. The question trial allows the students to generate questions related to a specific topic and to specify the directions in which these questions are leading them. Also, by developing some trial questions and organizing them into a particular strategy, students can ascertain if the questions are following accurately the strategy intended. In this activity, students procure information by which they assess the importance of their initial questions in relation to the strategy selected.

THE ACTIVITY. Basically, students organize themselves into teams with the first task to generate questions and put them into a strategy plan before actual investigation of a class topic. After creating these questions, students then talk over their questions with a teammate and obtain reactions as to whether the questions are at the intended cognitive level and whether they are sequenced in a manner appropriate to the guidelines of the chosen strategy. The teammate serving as reactor has to indicate the reasons for her reactions and to supply suggestions as to how the other individual can improve her questions, if such improvement is indicated. Since both teammates serve the role of reactor they gain practice in responding to questions and in relating them to particular strategies. When questions and strategies have been judged as productive, the student commences the "official" investigation.

Question Trial Sheet

MAJOR QUESTIONS TO BE CONSIDERED	JUDGMENT OF QUESTIONS
1._____	_____
2._____	_____
3._____	_____
4._____	_____

Suggestions for improving questions:

_____

_____

_____

Question sequence, question strategy formation:

ORIGINAL SEQUENCE	REACTIONS TO SEQUENCE
1._____	
2._____	

The adjusted sequence of questions (in relation to a particular strategy):

_____

_____

_____

Note. The question sequence can be indicated with numbers rather than writing out each question.

Example. Students in a city might be interested in analyzing the development of cities with regard to urban planning or lack of it. Using this topic focus, a student team might generate the following Trial Sheet.

Question Trial Sheet

MAJOR QUESTIONS TO BE CONSIDERED	JUDGMENT OF QUESTIONS
1. What is the definition of a city?	All right to focus attention.

2. How many cities are there in   All right for data base, but does
   the country?   not tell too much.
3. What are some of the key   Good, gets at analysis.
   characteristics of cities?

Suggestions for improving questions:
   Need to pose questions that will focus my attention on using
knowledge rather than just gathering facts.

QUESTION SEQUENCE, QUESTION STRATEGY FORMATION

ORIGINAL SEQUENCE   REACTIONS TO SEQUENCE

_____1_____   Needs some adjusting

_____2_____

_____3_____

ADJUSTED SEQUENCE
OF QUESTIONS

_____1_____   Don't really need question two at
                                     all to answer my major question.
_____3_____

CONCLUDING NOTES

The activities presented in this chapter have focused on the second
major phase of processing information, the doing or implementing phase. The central thrust of the activities is to have the students use the questions either in strategies or in particular
activities designed for application of skills in questioning. Some
of the activities related to preliminary stages of using questions,
such as the last activity.

Several of the games suggested get the student involved in
utilizing questions at specific cognitive and affective levels rather
than actually employing them in any particular strategy.

The activities contained in this chapter complement the strategies suggested in chapter 4 dealing with planning. As indicated
previously actions will be utilized in a sequence going from
planning, to using, to assessing.

No attempt was made to put these activities into any type of
sequence for there really is no basis for setting up an optimal
sequence. Which ones are employed first depends in part upon

the needs and interests of the students and the directional thrust of the lesson. Also, some of the situations, such as those relating to the actual incorporation of questions within a strategy, e.g., activity 3, will be used much more than others.

NOTES

1. FRANCIS P. HUNKINS, *Questioning Strategies and Techniques* (Boston: Allyn and Bacon, 1972), pp. 101-105 for more details.

2. BARBARA WARD, *Five Ideas that Change the World* (W. W. Norton & Company, Inc., 1959).

3. Ibid, p. 123.

4. CAROLINE T. GILLIN, MARCELLA L. KYSILHA, VIRGINIA M. ROGERS, and LEWIS B. SMITH, *Questioneze* (Columbus, Ohio: Charles E. Merrill Publishing Co., 1972).

5. Ibid, p. 31.

6. O. L. DAVIS and FRANCIS P. HUNKINS, *Asking about the USA and Its Neighbors* (New York: American Book Company, 1971), p. 2.

7. J. RICHARD SUCHMAN, *Developing Inquiry* (Chicago: Science Research Associates, Inc., 1966).

6

Involving Students in
Assessing Questions and
Questioning Strategies

INTRODUCTION

This chapter contains activities to involve students in the third stage of working with questions, assessing. Students need skill in assessing their questions for competent diagnosis furnishes data about whether questioning behavior should be maintained, altered, or stopped. In brief, it supplies feedback on the effectiveness of the learner's processing of information. Also, students need competence in judging the questions of others whether they are encountered in written materials or in speech.

The encounters in this chapter reflect a dual emphasis on assessing one's own questions and/or assessing other's questions. The activities also deal with evaluating the learner's questions at two stages: before actual use, such as critiquing

173

plans, and during and after use for in-class and out-of-class investigations.

To be engaged successfully in the following assessing activities, students must understand the nature and reason for assessment. The teacher should schedule discussions with his or her class regarding the role of assessment in relation to the three stages of processing information. Additionally, the teacher must plan formal lessons on criteria requisite for judging the value of questions and particular strategies. The teacher must also manage situations in which students can discover for themselves criteria for assessing questions and strategies.

Lessons in the use of specific assessment-observation schedules can be provided for students in order to assist them in accomplishing the activities suggested in this chapter.

The teacher needs to orchestrate student encounters with these activities so students are cognizant of the nature of and types of questions and comprehend the means by which they can engage in assessment.

The activities are discussed in the same format as used in the previous two chapters. Again, no attempt is made to present an optimal sequence of these means of involving students, for sequence depends upon teacher and student goals.

ASSESSING ACTIVITIES

Assessing Activity 1: Judging Your Own Questions

BASIC RATIONALE. Students and even their teachers fail to take time to analyze their questions. Just what types of questions do I use most often? Why do I ask the questions I do? Will the questions I raise really provide me with meaningful results?

Assessing Activity 1 enables learners to take stock of the questions they have used in the previous stages of planning and using. They can critique at this juncture if the questions extant in their planning are actually utilized in class investigation. To achieve this learners will need audio recordings, but recording their class dialogue is a good habit. Recording provides insight into the learners' information processing and facilitates the growth of student independence in the world of learning.

This activity also can foster critical mindedness, which is essential if increased skill in learning is to be forthcoming.

THE ACTIVITY. Have students contemplate a particular topic for investigation allowing them five or ten minutes to record four or five questions they think important to the focus. After listing the questions on a supplied form, have classmates share their thoughts with class colleagues. At this time, students can react to whether their questions are really effective or ineffective in relation to the topic. Have my questions really directed me in meaningful directions? Have my questions just centered on facts? Have my questions demanded some type of evaluation of data gathered? Should I revise my questions? If so, in what ways?

A format such as the following could be used:

Assessment Sheet Format

TOPIC:

Five significant questions:

1. _____
2. _____
3. _____
4. _____
5. _____

REACTIONS	LEVEL	IMPORTANCE	EFFECTIVENESS IN GETTING DESIRED INFORMATION
Question 1	_____	_____	_____
Question 2	_____	_____	_____
Question 3	_____	_____	_____
Question 4	_____	_____	_____
Question 5	_____	_____	_____

Overall reactions to my questions: _____
_____
_____

Example. Many classrooms have terrariums and students often spend considerable time observing them. A terrarium can serve as a focus for generating questions which can then be evaluated as to type and worth. Worth in this sense relates to whether the questions possess the potential to stimulate additional questions and to guide inquiry in productive directions. It relates to a quality of questions that we refer to as dynamism.

Inform the members of your class that they are to contemplate the terrarium and write five questions they consider significant and record them on a format sheet. After doing this, have them judge each question as to its cognitive and affective levels, implied importance, and whether on reconsideration they feel their questions are of value.

Such critiquing by a student might produce a format sheet filled in as follows.

Assessment Sheet, My Questions

TOPIC: Science, Terrarium

Five Significant Questions:
1. What plants are growing in the terrarium?
2. Identify any animals in the terrarium.
3. How much water does the terrarium have?

4. From what source do the plants obtain their food?
5. What might happen if more water were added?

REACTIONS	LEVEL	IMPORTANCE	EFFECTIVENESS
Question One	Knowledge	Yes	Provides information for finding out what type of terrarium one has
Question Two	Knowledge	Not too much	Just tells facts
Question Three	Knowledge	Not too much	Again, just stressing facts
Question Four	Knowledge	Not much	Just knowledge, does not really relate to this terrarium
Question Five	Comprehension	Somewhat	Gets at understanding, some inference making.

Overall reactions to my questions:
My questions are stressing knowledge too much.

Class involvement does not have to be conducted in precisely this manner. Quite often, rather than having the questions thought up and then analyzed, the questions can be taken from previous lesson situations. Perhaps the questions are those from student's plans or questions employed and recorded in a previous investigation. The major point is that time should be scheduled for students to assess their questions.

Assessing Activity 2:
Question Self-Analysis

BASIC RATIONALE. Question self-analysis is very similar to the previous student involvement, but differs in degree of structure. It is not geared to getting a readout on questions relating to a specific aspect of a topic at one point in time, but is aimed at critiquing a sample of students' questions during the course of a school day or class period. The thrust of the self-analysis is to obtain insights into types of questions students are asking or the types of questions to which they are responding. Students frequently discover that they respond only to questions representing particular types, while avoiding other types. The activity can be geared to both cognitive and affective domains.

THE ACTIVITY. Inform students that they are to keep a question self-analysis by taping their verbal responses in a particular class or a portion of several class periods. At designated periods of time, they will listen to these tapes and record on a document, similar to the following one, their questions, or the questions to which they have responded and then will determine the cognitive or affective levels of these questions. Then, the learners will evaluate their dealings with class questions.

Question Self-Analysis

FIRST FIVE-MINUTE SAMPLE OF MY QUESTIONS	RAISED	RESPONDED	TYPE
Question 1_____			
Question 2_____			
Question 3_____			

SECOND FIVE-MINUTE SAMPLE	RAISED	RESPONDED	TYPE
Question 1_____			

Question 2 _____

_____   _____   _____   _____

Overall Reactions_____

_____

_____

Students can obtain as many samples as they feel necessary to furnish an adequate picture of their questioning
behavior. In some sessions, they may find they ask few
questions, which is valuable information for them, while in
other sessions they may discover they participated most
energetically, but that their questions clustered at one particular cognitive level.

Students should acquire some information relating to the
effectiveness of their class participation. If they carry out
self-analysis over several types of classes and for several class
periods, they can ascertain if they partake more actively in
certain classes than in others. Students also can realize if
they are raising any questions for class consideration or if
they are merely responding when the teacher calls on them.

The same information can be obtained using an alternative format such as the Participation Checksheet.

My Participation Checksheet
_____

Questions I raised:

_____

_____

_____

Questions to which I responded:

_____

_____

My reactions to questions raised:

_____

My reactions to questions to which I responded:

General reactions, suggested future behavior with regard to my raising
and reacting to questions:

Example. Envision a lesson in reading at the intermediate grade level in which pupils are reading short stories
about early America. Pupils are taking five-minute samples
of their questions and questioning behavior. The result of
one such analysis appears below.

Question Self-Analysis

FIVE-MINUTE SAMPLE OF MY QUESTIONS	RAISED	RESPONDED	TYPE
Who was the main character?		*	Knowledge
Did Jack solve his problem?		*	Comprehension
Would I like to know Jack?	*		Responding

SECOND FIVE-MINUTE SAMPLE OF MY QUESTIONS	RAISED	RESPONDED	TYPE
(Note: These are from a different day.)			
Do I recognize the main message of the author?	*		Analysis
Was this a very effective story?	*		Evaluation Valuing

Would I read the story
   again?   *   Valuing

Overall reaction:
   My questions were better on the second sampling. Also, I raised
more questions than the first time.

   Such a self-check sheet provides the pupil with data
about whether he is responding to teacher questions and
what types of questions he is raising. Over several periods,
the pupil can begin to see if he has a preference for particular
kinds of questions and also if he shuns questions he considers
more difficult.

   Of course, the samplings can be longer than five minutes
and can be taken as often as the student wishes. The pupil
can develop profiles of his questioning behavior within particular subject areas using this activity.

   Example.   Students taking industrial arts, either for
their main area of study or for enrichment, should be conscious of the types of questions they generate as they work
and study in particular areas. For example, consider a class
at the junior high level working in graphic arts, specifically
block printing. Rather than having the teacher tell the students about all of the proper techniques for block printing,
the teacher informs the class that she is going to let them
experiment with the materials to discover for themselves how
to make effective block prints. In this example, relating to
the work of one student, the alternative format sheet is
used.

My Participation Check Sheet

QUESTIONS I RAISED:
   What type of design do I wish to make? What materials do I have
available? How long do I have to do this print?

QUESTIONS TO WHICH I RESPONDED:
   I responded to the first three questions to get me started. I sketched out my design and then identified a soft wood block I could use. I found out that I had five periods to work on this project.

MY REACTIONS TO THESE QUESTIONS:
   My questions allowed me to get "on target" with the lesson objective of creating a block print for exhibit.

OTHER QUESTIONS I RAISED:
   I raised the following questions as I was cutting the design on the wood block. How deeply do I need to make my cuts? Describe the texture of the paper on which I will make my block impression.
   How can I use my cutting tools to create a "rustic" or rough texture on the final print?
   I must think of the effect that light or heavy pressure will have on the block I am creating.

MY RESPONSES:
   I responded to all of these questions. To get answers to some of them, I inked the block at various times during the carving to determine if the design cut out was deep enough. I also tried the block with different types of paper and varying amounts of ink because of my last two questions.

MY REACTIONS TO MY QUESTIONS:
   I really liked my questions, for they helped me to experiment with the materials. I had fun experimenting.

OVERALL REACTIONS:
   My questions really helped me to create a block print I really liked. I also have learned more about the techniques of cutting and inking.

   Note. This question self-analysis activity allowed the student not only to be somewhat more creative, but made him more conscious of the procedures he was using. Also, it focused his attention on the reasons for his actions.
   Such assessment enables a student to gain an even greater knowledge of the content field in which he is working.
   Additionally, such an activity can allow him to increase his understanding of ways to process information, ways to

monitor his application of his knowledge. Having time to ask "Hey, what am I doing? What is the effect of what I am doing? Is there another way to do this?" provides students with valuable insights into the world of process learning. Of course, for the student to be so engaged assumes that he or she has studied, both formally and informally, several types of questions in both domains.

Assessing Activity 3: Attitude Check on Questions

BASIC RATIONALE. It is possible for students to spend their entire school years without determining their attitude or attitudes regarding types of questions and ways to use questions. Students commonly state their dislike of certain subjects, but it is rare that we hear them express their dissatisfaction or satisfaction with questions experienced in school. Youth need to consider major types of questions and to indicate their affective responses to questions. Do they value the question as important, or worthwhile? Do they realize that questions can facilitate productive inquiry? Do they consider the question as a potential threat to their values? Do they believe questions can enable one to obtain a more complete view of the world? Do they enjoy reacting to questions that leave them with additional, unanswered points?

This attitude check gives classmates time to reflect upon how they react affectively to particular types of questions, in both domains.

THE ACTIVITY. Have learners record ten questions they deal with over a week's time and indicate their reactions to these questions. A second reaction can be required if the teacher feels this will provide the student with a better insight.

The questions listed can be learner-originated or ones initially posed by the teacher or even contained in some of the materials used in class. A form for this activity follows.

Attitude Check on Questions

QUESTIONS RAISED, CONSIDERED	INITIAL ATTITUDE REACTION	SECOND REACTION
1. _____	_____	_____
2. _____	_____	_____
3. _____	_____	_____
4. _____	_____	_____
5. _____	_____	_____
6. _____	_____	_____
7. _____	_____	_____
8. _____	_____	_____
9. _____	_____	_____
10. _____	_____	_____

General reactions to my attitude/s regarding questions, types of questions. _____
_____
_____
_____

Example.   The example relates to a lesson at the secondary level dealing with environment, specifically the relationship of man, food, and environment. The major objective of the lesson is to enable students to understand that man currently is using most of the arable land and that solutions to problems of food production lie not in increasing acreage, but in improving productivity on existing lands. The thrust of the lesson has directed class members to consider just how committed they are to helping developing nations of the world meet their food needs. The commitment issue is checked by having individuals list questions raised and considered and their reactions to these questions. Some of these questions may have been teacher initiated.

A partial result of one student's analysis follows.

Attitude Check on Questions

QUESTIONS RAISED, CONSIDERED	INITIAL REACTION	SECOND REACTION
How much land is available for food production?	Interest	Interest
Do we have sufficient land in food production to meet our immediate and distant needs?	Concern	Concern, not really worried.
What would I do to improve the food supply?	Nothing really.	I am not sure, but most likely leave it to others to solve.
What plans can I suggest to increase food supply?	Willing to listen to views of others.	Willing to leave problems to others.
Do I have an obligation to help in the solution to this problem?	No	I suppose I could eat less of some things.

General reaction to my attitude regarding these questions:
I have interest in the facts relating to the issue, but I really do not have interest in determining what action I should take. I feel that I should only deal with issues I can realistically process.

This particular individual was not too concerned with problems not affecting him directly. However, on second reaction, he did express some ambivalence as to whether he should be concerned with the issue and come up with some plans. However, the student did register that he was interested in the topic, but not really committed to action. He was willing to leave that to others.

Over several class periods, the student can determine if he has an attitude reflected in his questions related to this issue. It is evident that this activity is aimed primarily at the affective domain.

Assessing Activity 4: Criteria
Check on My Questions

BASIC RATIONALE. Individuals often ask and respond to questions aiming at being correct or eliciting a "good" from the teacher. However, students need time to consider questions planned for particular investigations or questions raised and recorded in class sessions and to judge these questions against criteria for good questions. Then they can develop the ability to criticize their own questions, which is requisite to improving questioning.

THE ACTIVITY. The criteria check calls for students to sample their questions in specific subject areas over a period of time, usually a few days. The students have a list of criteria supplied by the teacher, developed by themselves, or developed cooperatively with peers. The criteria are listed along the top of a page and the questions are indicated along the side. Students check their questions against the indicated criteria. Students may wish to share their results with the teacher or with other classmates. Merely listing and checking questions is not productive; learners need opportunities to discourse with others regarding just how their questions measure up.

Criteria Check on My Questions

CRITERIA	1	2	3	4	5	6	7	8	9
QUESTION SAMPLE									
1. _____									
2. _____									
3. _____									
4. _____									
5. _____									
6. _____									

General Reactions to Questions:

_____

_____

_____

_____

Criteria:
1. Do questions relate to the objectives of the lesson?
2. Do the questions trigger my interests?
3. Do the questions lead me to questions at higher levels?
4. Do the questions allow me to work with materials?
5. Are the questions feasible in terms of time?
6. Are the questions clearly worded?
7. Are the questions capable of leading me to form concepts and generalizations?
8. Are the questions clear as to cognitive level?
9. Are the questions clear as to affective level?

Note. Not all questions need to satisfy these criteria, but the overall sample of questions should meet the majority of these criteria. You can adjust the format of the sheet to suit the specific requirements of the class. The important point is that pupils have some means of checking their questions.

Example. The criteria checksheet of a student's questions was prepared in a secondary level economic class dealing with personal income distribution.

Criteria Check on My Questions

QUESTION (SAMPLING)	1	2	3	4	5	6	7	8	9
1. What is the average income of farm workers?	✓	✓			✓	✓		✓	
2. Why is per capita income lower in some states than in others?	✓	✓			✓	✓	✓	✓	

3. Distinguish the ill effects of great disparity in the distribution of personal incomes.	✓	✓	✓	✓	✓	✓	✓	✓	✓
4. Create a plan to reduce the disparity in incomes.	✓	✓	✓	✓		✓	✓	✓	✓

General Reactions to Questions:
Most of my questions met a majority of the criteria. However, some of the questions (1, 2) were not very powerful. They only enabled me to get some facts. The question on creating a plan really is not possible with the class time allotted.

In completing and reviewing this checksheet the student obtains a fairly good indication of the types of questions she is raising and their quality. This example is perhaps somewhat unrealistic for no student is going to formulate questions that will meet most criteria at first, but, after working with questions, such high quality questions should be possible.

As with several other assessment activities, the student needs to cultivate the behavior of recording her questions on audiotape or jotting down her questions, at least the major ones, in a notebook for later analysis.

Assessing Activity 5: Question Problem Identification

BASIC RATIONALE. Some learners just can't seem to get with it, and reasons for their inaction often elude both student and teacher. However, to be an effective questioner learners need an accurate assessment of their questioning behavior. Analysis of behavior can uncover certain difficulties needing correction. Students may be having problems responding to questions at particular cognitive levels or may be unwilling to respond to questions at certain affective levels. Perhaps pupils encounter uncertainty in generating questions at particular levels more so than responding to specific question types. Or learners may be in a quandary when attempting to identify questions significant to a particular investigation's focus.

Problem identification relates to models of teaching aimed at assisting students to comprehend themselves better. Here the focus is on understanding themselves specifically as students although people cannot learn about themselves in the questioning dimension without gaining some insight into their total personality.

THE ACTIVITY. Give class members a form on which to record in general terms their perceived problems in dealing with questions. If learners feel they have no problems, they can either not engage in this activity or they can develop a report indicating the strong points of their questioning. The teacher should provide time for either teacher-student or student-student debriefing. Ways to eliminate problems identified need to be advanced and a timetable arranged for carrying out the procedure for improvement of questions.

Question Problem Identification

Problems, difficulties with questions:

_____

_____

_____

_____

Reasons for the problems:

_____

_____

_____

_____

Plausible ways to eliminate the problem:

_____

_____

_____

_____

Example. Students in a mathematics class at the upper intermediate level are provided time in which to query themselves about whether they have any problems posing questions in this area and if so, to indicate as specifically as possible what they are. For our example the class is dealing with word problems. With this focus, a problem identification for an individual might be filled out as follows.

Question Problem Identification

PROBLEMS, DIFFICULTIES WITH QUESTIONS:
My problem is that the questions I ask to help me solve the problem don't really help me. I still have a hard time figuring out the correct way to get the answer.

REASONS FOR PROBLEMS:
I don't think I allow myself enough time to ask questions at the application and analysis levels. I ask lots of knowledge level questions which get me facts, but don't allow me to see how all the facts fit together.

PLAUSIBLE WAYS TO ELIMINATE THE PROBLEM:
I need to take more time with the problem. Perhaps I can work with a friend and see if she can help me ask application questions so I can apply what I know.

When students first do this, they will most likely require assistance from the teacher or a paraprofessional to gain this insight, but in time, pupils should become fairly adept at diagnosing their problems. Again, the teacher should accept the assumption that if given assistance, students can manage much of their own learning.

> *Assessing Activity 6: Determining Depth of Knowledge Regarding Questions*

BASIC RATIONALE. Occasionally when working with questions, learners should ask, "Just how much do I know about questions, my questions, strategies, my use of strategies?" They need to administer a self-test on how knowledgeable they are. Testing is a milestone event for it provides students with data that allow them to continually perfect their knowledge of questions and their skills of questioning.

As indicated in the model of processing information, assessing is connected to the stages of planning and implementation via feedback loops. This particular assessing activity also should be used in the planning stage of information processing to determine the current level of student understanding regarding questions prior to investigating a topic. Indeed, this activity can be used as a criteria measure to identify clearly those needs students have regarding their comprehension and skill in using questions. The teacher can use the Knowledge Depth Test to assess student understanding in order to determine how much formal teaching is necessary regarding questions.

The activity should provide information relating to the student's knowledge of questions both in the cognitive and affective domains as well as data relating to which strategies he knows and those on which he needs further study and practice. This engagement could relate to the behavior modification model, for the student, upon discovering his strengths and weaknesses, can outline means of altering his behavior to correct the weakness.

THE ACTIVITY. A major way to assess this depth of knowledge is to develop a test in which students are queried on various aspects of questions about types, purpose, dimensions, and procedures for assessment. The teacher can develop essay-type questions to which the learner must respond. It is not the purpose here to develop a test which the teacher can administer to a class; the point is to provide a general idea of ways to determine a student's degree of comprehension in the realm of questions.

Knowledge Depth Regarding Questions

Identify the following question types as to their cognitive and affective levels.

_____

_____

_____

If you were to investigate topic_____what would be three major questions you would want to ask. Indicate why you select these questions.

_____

_____

_____

Assume you are investigating topic_____ and have confronted a primary source dealing with the original conflict. Delineate the types of questions that could provide you with the most usable information.

_____

_____

_____

What procedures would you employ? Determine whether you have generated productive questions.

_____

_____

_____

_____

Note. This assessing for knowledge does not need to be written. The teacher can question students orally, and often chatting about questions puts pupils more at ease and perhaps provides a more accurate picture of their understanding. It should be stressed that this activity is not for a grade, but only to provide data to give learners an accurate "picture" of their level of questioning and means by which they might improve their use of questions in processing information.

Assessing Activity 7: Analyzing Questions in Speech

BASIC RATIONALE. Students spend a lot of time talking with the teacher and classmates, and educational researchers have devoted much time to analyzing classroom speech to gain insight into teaching. It seems most productive for learners to realize that speech analysis can provide meaningful information. Most of our speech is declarative in nature, but much of the declarative verbalization is triggered by teacher questions.

It may be most meaningful for students to determine the interrogative nature of their discourse and then to delimit the types of questions they utilize in their classroom and out-of-class speech. Activity 7 seems to be a productive exercise by which students can ascertain the ratio of interrogative to declarative speech and then to specify the types of questions reacted to or produced. This analysis may also reveal extant relationships between statements and particular questions. Students do raise questions and do make statements relating to these questions, and this verbalization should be investigated to enable the learner to grasp a "handle" relating to his or her verbal functioning. This analysis will enable the student to become a more effective learner, a more aware questioner.

THE ACTIVITY. The activity requires pupils to audiotape their speech, record the total ratio of questions to statements, and then indicate the specific questions dealt with by cognitive or affective type. The degree of depth for this analysis depends upon the level of schooling. From such a sampling, students can make a profile of their questioning behavior regarding question types they utilized or reacted to. A chart could graph the quantity of questions raised during a class period.

Questions in My Speech

Number of statements per unit time: _____

Number of questions per unit time: _____

LEVELS OF QUESTIONS RAISED	NO. OF QUESTIONS AT THIS LEVEL
Know	_____
Comp	_____
Apply	_____
Analy	_____
Syn	_____
Evalu	_____
Attend	_____
Respond	_____
Value	_____
Org	_____
Char	_____

General impressions of my questions: _____

_____

_____

Suggestions for adjustment of questioning behavior:

_____

_____

_____

CHARTING OF MY QUESTIONS

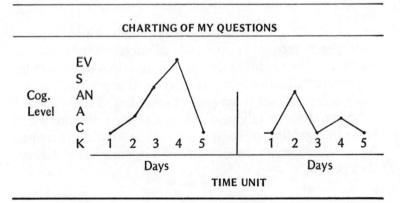

Note. A similar charting can be done for affective questions. Some students may find this way of recording their questioning behavior meaningful. Also, it might be useful to students to keep charts over a period of time to determine if their questions change as a result of more information and greater understanding of questions.

Assessing Activity 8: Matching Questions with Goals, Objectives

BASIC RATIONALE. For a student to determine the effectiveness of his functioning he must have clear goals indicated and attendant objectives developed and time to consider if his questions match the intent of objectives and/or goals. Regarding questioning, objectives have two dimensions: the process dimension, that of asking particular types of questions in certain sequences or strategies; and the content dimension, relating to specific content or subject matter that one is to process via questioning.

THE ACTIVITY. Suppose students have developed clear process and content objectives for themselves. Have them develop charts with three columns in which they first record their objectives; second, list their major questions; and third, indicate whether they think the questions relate to or enable them to achieve intended objectives.

Example. If you were engaging learners in a social studies lesson on pollution, students perhaps would have generated the following objective, "From studying this unit on pollution, I will be able to explain what pollution is and give at least two examples of each of the major types of pollution as evident in my community." The learners enter this objective in their first column. Then, either through listening to tapes or analyzing their written papers, they indicate some of the major questions they raised relating to this objective. For instance, pupil "A" may discover that she asked the following three questions relating to pollution: "What do experts in the field of pollution feel are the major causes of pollution? What types of pollution are listed in my textbook? Is there a relationship between the type of industry in an area and the type of pollution?" These questions are recorded on this chart and the student, either alone or with a teammate, judges whether these queries have or will enable her to achieve the objectives set for herself. A form such as the following could be used.

Matching Questions with Objectives

MAJOR OBJECTIVES	QUESTIONS	PLUS OR MINUS
From studying this unit on pollution, I will be able to explain what pollution is.	What do experts in the field of pollution feel are major causes of pollution?	+
Give two examples	What types of pollution are listed in my textbook?	−
As evident in my community	Is there a relationship between the type of industry in the area and the type of pollution?	+

General reactions to my questions:
    My first two questions lead me to my general objective, but I need questions relating to analyzing types of pollution evident in my community, and also questions relating to types of industry. Such questions will help me isolate an example of pollution in my community.

        Note. This matching can be done with any subject area. If you were conducting a lesson in art, the learner might have the objective to develop a collage using various types of fabrics to depict the sense of motion and conflict. The student would need questions such as "What types of fabrics have interesting texture? What is the affect of texture on various persons? What are some basic rules of composition? How does composition and balance relate to theme in art? Does what I have done have balance according to criteria established in this class?"

Such questions would be recorded in the second column and the student would then check a plus or minus indicating if the questions were guiding him or her toward the creation of the desired collage.

One can also use this activity as a planning activity. Students can indicate the major objectives for themselves and list questions they would like to ask. They then can determine if these questions have sufficient potential to facilitate the attainment of the stated objectives. In this way non-productive questions can be eliminated before the actual investigation.

Assessing Activity 9: Judging Teacher's Questions

BASIC RATIONALE. Learning occurs either in a dyadic situation involving the student with another student or material or in a triadic situation involving the learner with some type of material or media or student and the teacher.[1] This can be graphically shown as

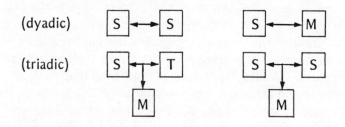

In those situations in which a student or several students are interacting with the teacher, it can be beneficial for students to analyze the questions of their teacher. Such analysis can enable learners to become mqre adept at recognizing

question types which can contribute to their general knowledge of questions and questioning.

THE ACTIVITY. Activity 9 consists of recording a lesson in which the teacher has assumed a major role. This would be a triadic teaching-learning situation. The learners tape the teacher's questions and after the lesson indicate the questions identifying their cognitive or affective types. After this coding, they synthesize their general reactions to the teacher's questions. It is important to stress that this is not an evaluative exercise in which students are afforded an opportunity to judge whether the teacher is doing an effective job. Rather, students have a learning experience in which to gain practice in question recognition using the teacher as exemplar. Of course the teacher needs to be a skilled questioner if this activity is to have benefit for learners.

Example. Consider a science lesson in botany at either the elementary or secondary level dealing with growth characteristics of plants. The teacher introduces the lesson by reviewing the major features of flowering plants. A bean plant is used as an example. The teacher, as part of this review, asks "What are the major parts of this bean plant? Explain the function of the stem. What purpose does the leaf serve? Indicate how photosynthesis takes place in the plant. What is needed for photosynthesis to occur?"

The students record the cognitive level of these questions. Learners also assess how much they understand about the plant. The teacher should keep in mind that class members are interested both in their questions and their level of understanding and use of information. Once these questions have been classified by level, students can indicate the major directions of the lesson. They might even hypothesize why the teacher is using these questions. The hypothesizing could be checked later in a dialogue with the teacher as to his or her intent.

Students then might experiment with various bean plants in controlled situations. For example, class members could place one bean plant in bright sunlight, another in reduced sunlight and at an angle, another in shade, and another in darkness. The teacher could raise the following questions: describe the present condition of your bean plant. What happened during the first day of your experiment? Describe how the plant reacted to the existing condition. What general statements can you make regarding the plants' reaction to the conditions described? Would other members of the class agree with these conclusions?

These questions can be listed on a form similar to the one below.

Judging Teacher's Questions

TEACHER'S QUESTIONS	COGNITIVE/ AFFECTIVE LEVELS
1. What are the major parts of a plant?	K
2. Explain the function of the stem.	C
3. What purpose does the leaf serve?	K
4. Indicate how photosynthesis takes place in plants.	C
5. Describe the present condition of your plant.	C
9. Describe the reactions of the plant to the existing conditions.	C
10. What general statements can you make?	Syn

General reactions to teacher's questions:

The teacher spent a major part of the initial session dealing with knowledge and comprehension questions. These questions helped us review. Later questions asked us to report what we did and observed and to draw conclusions and then to evaluate our statements.

The stress here is on increasing student awareness of types of questions, improving student skill in recognizing question types, and facilitating learner competence in responding to questions at the levels intended by the teacher. In short, this activity aims at enabling learners to maximize their learning when reacting to their teacher's questions.

Assessing Activity 10: Judging the Questions of Notable Persons

BASIC RATIONALE. Sometimes by focusing on the questions of experts, students can ascertain the depth of attention required for reading or listening to "authorities." This activity, similar to the previous one, allows learners to sharpen their awareness of questions and refine the manner in which they process content of authorities communicated by various media. Also, focusing on questions can facilitate the identification of what is truly important.

THE ACTIVITY. Have students select a recognized authority in some field and listen to particular speeches or read some of his writings. Learners read or listen with two purposes: to determine the types of questions this person uses, either explicitly or implicitly, and to obtain additional information on specific topics. These major questions can be recorded, indicating the cognitive/affective levels of the questions, with the major thrust of the questions identified. Of course, not all questions raised by the person need to be recorded or analyzed, but the question sample should be adequate enough to enable the student to formulate general conclusions.

Example. Assume a lesson within the content field of language arts in which the class is investigating the use of language in today's culture and the effect of media on the written word. Students are assigned a language authority's book and are to delineate stated or implied questions. The activity could result in a listing similar to that recorded in this language arts form.

Judging Questions

TOPIC AREA: Language Arts
FOCUS: The use of language in today's culture

MAJOR QUESTIONS	LEVEL OF QUESTIONS	PURPOSE
1. What are some major uses of language in today's world?	Knowledge	Focus readers' attention
2. How many people today read more than a book a year?	Knowledge	Focus readers' attention on change in language usage
3. How have you used language in the last month?	Comprehension Valuing	Relate topic to individual. Get at the reader's value base regarding his use of language.
4. Based on the current scene, predict some ways in which media will serve as an extension of man's language.	Synthesis	Wishes reader to synthesize information read, and to make some predictions. Also used as a means to get reader to determine how complete his or her understanding of language is. Gives reader chance to use language to express understanding.

General reactions to questions:
I felt the writer overemphasized knowledge questions. He should have raised more questions directing our attention to the relationships existing among uses of language and modes of media. He could have directed us to make judgments as to accuracy of his predictions. Still, the questions got me somewhat interested in the topic.

Note. Of course, these are hypothetical questions. It is possible that some individuals may never raise any questions specifically, but only allude to major questions pertinent to his area of expertise. However, it is valuable for persons to be skilled in inferring questions from positions assumed by authorities.

Judging questions can be used in any subject area and grade level. Classmates might be concerned with such social issues as racial relations and delineate major positions being advocated to enhance race relations. The topic of international peace could be investigated via the analysis of the stands authorities make and the questions they emphasize. Scholars who have won prizes can be the targets for question analysis. What questions have concerned major historians? What questions were raised regarding the making of a President? The list is limitless.

Assessing Activity 11:   Checking Questions on TV

BASIC RATIONALE. The two previous engagements centered on getting students cognizant of the types of questions individuals use. This activity is similar in purpose, differing only in that it centers learners' attention on a medium dominating a large part of young peoples' lives, television.

Repeatedly, learners process information received via TV in an uncritical, unquestioning manner; they just listen with the purpose of remembering what was said, thus ignoring the need to analyze the assumptions, the values behind some of the information discussed as well as the implications of positions taken. Of course, this activity is not focusing on programs designed primarily for entertainment, such as a "comedy" special or the local mystery theater. Rather this discussion relates to programs such as serious talk shows, specials dealing with current issues, and programs on educational television. Even daily news programs can be analyzed by the questions raised by the commentators.

THE ACTIVITY. Have students develop record sheets on which to record the questions raised by persons appearing on television shows dealing with certain events. The class can be assigned to listen to the same program and monitor the questions generated. The result then can be considered in a debriefing session where students can discern if similar questions were noticed and classified in identical categories. Conclusions relating to the programs and the questions can be shared among class colleagues with perhaps schemes suggested for additional question analysis.

It is possible for students to follow a major event being discussed on TV over several programs to determine if questions raised require one to process information at levels other than knowledge and comprehension. Incidents such as Watergate, the use of germ warfare, racial problems, the use of resources, and the monetary crisis are frequently aired on television and can be considered for analysis.

Example. Suppose the Watergate episode is the focus for question analysis. Learners can concentrate on two or three major persons who were on the panel and record their questions. Are the questions only after facts? Are the questions aimed at discovering basic assumptions or violation of basic assumptions? Are the questions utilized to identify a pattern, a relationship among various events?

Questions on TV

TOPIC: Watergate hearings.
SUBJECT: Social Studies

QUESTIONS RAISED	COGNITIVE/ AFFECTIVE LEVEL
Individual No. 1's questions:	
1. Did you meet with the President?	K
2. What did the President say in reaction?	C
3. Would you say that there existed an awareness on the part of Mr. _____ as to what the other parties previously mentioned were doing?	An.

4. Would you say that what you did would   Ev.
   be considered illegal?

   Individual No. 2's questions:

1. When was the first meeting?   K
2. Put in your own words what you thought   C
   the President was saying.
3. Describe the nonverbal reactions of the   C
   President.
4. From your discussion with Mr. _____,   An.
   what was the major assumption
   he was making?
5. The *Washington Post* ran a story on   Ev.
   the event to which you alluded. Is that
   an accurate picture of what transpired?

General reactions to the questions:
   Both individuals raised questions at several cognitive levels. I felt
the questions were productive, and it was interesting to see how
lawyers use questions.

Note. These questions are fiction but they do provide
an example of plausible questions and how one might code
them. Such a task encourages students to become more
critical processors of information. Not only are they after
the facts, but they are using their awareness of questions to
judge whether the information being processed is relevant to
their purpose. Also, analysis of questions can provide exemplars of good questioning behavior.

*Assessing Activity 12: Question
Impact Test*

   BASIC RATIONALE. The impact test can serve a
double function: one of discerning the impact specific questions have on others; or two, of analyzing how certain
questions affect the asker. Either way the test relates primarily to the affective domain in that it is concerned with

the levels of how one responds, what values become evident in one's response, and how an individual's response relates to his total organization of information and perceptions of others.

Certainly, students should reflect on their reactions to questions. If this tack is taken, it is similar to the attitude check. However, students often need to be cognizant of how others react to certain types of questions. Quite often a person's reactions to questions reveal a great deal regarding her value system, the information she feels important, the assumption she has accepted and even her philosophical position in some instances.

Students should realize that some questions can antagonize individuals, others can make them apprehensive, some can cause people to withdraw from dialogue and personal interactions. Being able to recognize the impact of certain questions provides the student an edge on his interactions with others, whether they are fellow students or individuals from the community.

THE ACTIVITY. In this activity students create some type of check sheet for recording the questions and then the impact these questions have. The topic and the population considered are indicated as well as a place for conclusions and future action.

With the check sheet in hand, learners perhaps can begin by first observing the reactions of their fellow classmates. Not all students observe at the same time. Students can work in teams and share their perceptions and observations of particular individuals in the class. Reactions and prescriptions can be written up. Of course, the students being observed should be asked first for their permission.

After class members have become somewhat skilled in analyzing their friends, they can begin analyzing the questions of particular notables in the community. Each student would be assigned just one or two persons.

Example. Assume that students in a sex education class are to analyze how persons in the community react to particular questions stated or implied in dialogue of the school board relating to this curriculum area. A student with such a focus might generate a data sheet similar to the Question Impact Test.

Question Impact Test

TOPIC: Sex Education
POPULATION ANALYZED: Individuals in my community

QUESTIONS	REACTIONS
Individual No. 1	
1. Do our students need sex education?	Interest in question and response
2. Just what will be the subject areas covered?	Interest in question and response
3. How will the moral issue be covered?	Interest in question and some displeasure at the response
4. Will birth control be covered?	Concern evidenced at the question, and voiced opposition to the response and that it will be covered at all
5. Will these materials be used to discuss (sex) relations?	Anger at the response regarding how the material will be covered.
Individual No. 2	
1. _____	

General comments on individuals' reactions:
    Individual No. 1 was interested at first but exhibited concern when the questions and responses centered on discussing issues of birth control and sex relations. Individual seemed content to have simple knowledge questions handled, but opposed to having students making some conclusions regarding sex.

Individual No. 2 exhibited an attitude of interest throughout and did not appear threatened by any of the questions or resulting discussion.

I would predict that Individual No. 1 may produce some resistance to the sex education program in the community.

Note. Students can analyze how their classmates react to questions dealing with pollution, racism, economics, price and wage controls, the use of agricultural land for industrial purposes, the use of censorship in society, the quality of modern art, the use of science to prepare weapons, the use of algebra in our daily lives, using mathematical algorithms to make designs, the use of slang, the role of modern literature in the lives of classmates. The list is limitless.

Assessing Activity 13: Judging Questions and Questioning Strategies

BASIC RATIONALE. Students need to be knowledgeable about the nature of questions and various questioning strategies in order to gain information about realms of knowledge as well as about themselves. But in order to gain skill and competence in the use of process, learners require means of assessing their questions and their questioning strategies. This activity provides such a means for self-assessment and indicates to students the essence of evaluation to process learning.

THE ACTIVITY. This judging requires students either to audio or videotape themselves when employing questions in a particular strategy or to critique the questions recorded in their notes. The activity requires learners well versed in several strategies or models of processing data and cognizant of types of questions in both domains.

Judging Questioning Strategies

Questioning Strategy Utilized: _____

Questions used in strategy:	Judgment of Questions	Reason for Judgment
_____	_____	_____

Questions used in strategy:	Judgment of Questions	Reason for Judgment
_____	_____	_____
_____	_____	_____

Rating of the strategy as to its appropriateness for the particular topic investigated: _____

_____

_____

Elements of the strategy to be maintained: _____

_____

Elements of the strategy requiring improvement: _____

_____

Plausible ways to strengthen strategy and/or questions: _____

_____

_____

Example. Consider learners in the area of mathematics scheduled to use the Hunkins Combination Strategy which employs questions at several levels of Bloom's cognitive taxonomy with questions shifting from one cognitive level to another as required by the investigation. The strategy allows the learner to use questions to process information at increasingly higher cognitive levels. Affective levels are implied in the strategy.

Imagine that the learners are third graders just beginning to study the concept of probability. The teacher explains that he has six gumdrops in a box. Three are lemon, two orange, and one cherry. The teacher structures the lesson saying that the children are to ask questions to discover what will be their chances of getting particular flavors of gumdrops. Pupils work with a classmate, and the teacher encourages team members to ask as many questions as possible. The following chart might result from such a lesson. Of course, the working might be nearer the language of third grade children.

Combination Strategy Assessment

STRATEGY USED: Combination strategy

QUESTIONS USED IN STRATEGY	JUDGMENT	REASON FOR JUDGMENT
1. How many gumdrops are there?	OK	I find out how many candies there are.
2. How many of each flavor?	OK	Tells me something.
3. Do I like these flavors?	No good	Does not help me answer the teacher's major question.
4. What would happen if I take one from the box without looking? (Pupil does it?)	OK	Gets me to process information.
5. What flavor did I get?	OK	Provides information.
6. What flavor do I get if I try again? (Pupil does it.)	OK	Provides information.
7. Will I get more of one flavor than another?	Good	I like this one. Got me thinking about all the kinds of gumdrops.
8. Will I have a better chance of getting my favorite flavor if I eat one gumdrop?	Good	Suggests something to do.
9. I wonder what happens if I add another lemon gumdrop?	OK	Not sure why.

(Pupil then in a team tries to get
a lemon gumdrop and records
his success)

10. How many lemons did I get?	OK	Provides information.
11. Do I get more lemon gum-drops in four tries if I add more lemon drops to the box?	Good	Gets me thinking about gumdrops.
12. Does the number of each type of gumdrop help or hurt my chances of getting a particular flavor.	Good	Gets me thinking about how one can get better chances.

Rating of Strategy: I liked these questions, at least most of them.
Helped me thinking about numbers, also gumdrops.

Elements to be maintained: I think I would ask most of these
questions again.

Elements to be improved: I don't think I would ask the question
about flavor again.

Ways to improve my questions: I might ask the teacher if the questions
are good. Or, I could ask my friend if she liked my questions.

Note. The teacher may find that this lesson example
is not realistic regarding children at this level. However,
dealing with gumdrops certainly fits into the capabilities of
children at the concrete operational stages of mental development. Also, children whose teacher has discussed types of
questions and how questions help us would certainly be able
to ask questions. Of course, the wording might differ from
the example. Also, the teacher might have to provide a fairly
high degree of structure at first to guide children in their
questions. But if this type of experience were commonplace
in the classroom and children had ample opportunities for
working with questions, the example is most probable.
Children do ask questions and they begin to discern differences and relationships among various data whether they
are working with blocks, gumdrops, dots, or Arabic numerals.

Assessing Activity 14: Checking
the Ideal-Actual Levels of Questions

BASIC RATIONALE. One way to determine whether
questions are useful or not is to match those used against
those planned. There should be a high degree of agreement
between the questions students plan and those employed in
class. This particular activity allows students to assess this
agreement.

THE ACTIVITY. In planning particular means of processing
information, learners catalogue their major questions.
These questions are saved and during the processing of the
information, the students tape either their questions or just
the major questions in their notes. After completing a study
the investigators list the questions they actually used and jot
them down on the format sheet containing the originally
planned questions. The actual questions are lined up with
those originally planned, the ideal, and if there is agreement
at least regarding the major thrust of the questions asked
with questions planned, a plus is indicated. If little resemblance appears between the question asked and the one
planned, then a minus is recorded. In this way the student
can discern if he is actually following his plans. The format
could resemble the following one.

Ideal-Actual Levels of Questions

TOPIC: _____

IDEAL	ACTUAL	AGREEMENT
_____	_____	_____
_____	_____	_____
_____	_____	_____
_____	_____	_____

Overall Reactions:

_____

_____

_____

_____

_____

     Example. Imagine a class at the secondary level study-
ing the place of philosophy in human life, and investigating
the major views of reality held by particular philosophical
schools. The ideal-actual chart below indicates the questions
planned and actually asked by one student during this lesson.

Ideal-Actual Levels of Questions

TOPIC: Consideration of the major philosophies and how people
       utilize these stances in their lives.

IDEAL	ACTUAL	AGREE-MENT
What is the major view of reality of each philosophy?	How do the major philosophies view life?	+
Which philosophy considers man to be the prime processer of information?	Where does man assume the major problem-solving role?	+
How can I group these philosophies?	What are the likenesses and differences between existentialism and experimentalism?	+
How does each philosophy relate to man's view of education?	What type of education would each of these philosophies advocate?	+
What values are stressed by these philosophies?	How do these philosophies interpret good?	+

Overall reaction: I think my questions used in class investigation were
closely aligned with those planned.

Note. From an overview of this chart the student can see that the questions he asked clearly agreed with those he planned. Certainly they were not verbal duplicates, but script writing is not the function of this activity.

The degree of usefulness of this chart and activity depends upon the ability of the student to obtain a listing of the questions actually used in the classroom. If he has not taped his lesson, and has not indicated on notes or just does not recall the questions he used and the sequence, then he cannot use this assessment procedure.

Assessing Activity 15: Question Profile

BASIC RATIONALE. Students can attain readings of their immediate questioning behavior, but they also need feedback on the questioning over extended time periods to determine the productiveness of their questioning over many lessons and to get a measure on whether their questions and questioning skill are in fact improving over time due to their involvement with various process models. Anyone can pose good questions today, but not ask good questions tomorrow. A student can pose effective questions with this type of lesson or topic and not generate inductive questions in another area of study. Students need to resolve whether or not their questioning is constantly good and consistent across subject areas. This profile enables the student to check his questions and questioning behavior periodically in order to decide if his questioning quality is remaining at a steady state, or if it is improving or degenerating over time.

THE ACTIVITY. Learners are encouraged to take ten or fifteen minutes at various intervals, perhaps once a week, to indicate the major cognitive and/or affective levels of their questions relating to a specific subject area. This information is recorded on a chart similar to the profile question check denoting the date of the check and the cognitive and/or affective level of the majority of the questions evident. This check is repeated for as long as the student finds it useful. Students can make these checks for each domain in specific subject areas to obtain profiles of questions within these areas.

Profile Question Check

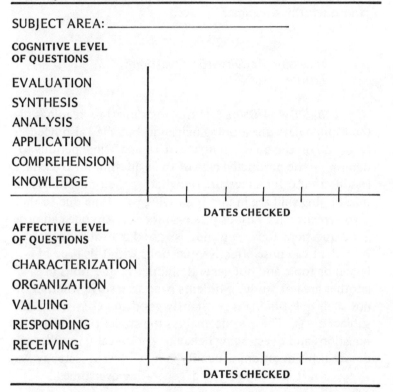

SUBJECT AREA: _____

COGNITIVE LEVEL
OF QUESTIONS

EVALUATION
SYNTHESIS
ANALYSIS
APPLICATION
COMPREHENSION
KNOWLEDGE

DATES CHECKED

AFFECTIVE LEVEL
OF QUESTIONS

CHARACTERIZATION
ORGANIZATION
VALUING
RESPONDING
RECEIVING

DATES CHECKED

Example. Consider students focusing on a lesson in economics comprising a three-week unit for dealing with the concept of market. The teacher is using structured discovery since materials and activities are organized so that students are directed to consider the concept of market rather than some other topic. However, the teacher does encourage the students to work in teams and to generate their own questions.

For the sake of the example, consider the questions of one student and suppose that her first question is "What types of things do I use every day?" She follows with "Do I need the things I get? Where do I get the things I need? Where is the best place to purchase these things?" These questions can be coded primarily at the knowledge level.

Several days later a check on her questions reveals her asking, "What causes people to buy certain goods and not others? Is there any relationship between the type of goods that an individual wants and how much he has to pay for it? What might happen if people stopped using these goods?" These questions are at least at the comprehension level.

A third check by the student, perhaps a week later, indicates the following questions. "If I were to stockpile a lot of goods, what might be the effect on the marketplace? What are some of the major assumptions that underlie the concept of market? How can I make the marketplace more productive with regard to my needs?" These questions are primarily at the analysis and synthesis level.

The recording of these questions on the graph would reveal the following profile.

Question Profile

SUBJECT AREA: Economics, the marketplace

COGNITIVE LEVEL

EVALUATION
SYNTHESIS
ANALYSIS
APPLICATION
COMPREHENSION
KNOWLEDGE

Day 1   Day 7   Day 14
DATES CHECKED

Note. Only the major question type used is indicated. Observation of the table provides the student with a clear indication that her questions are proceeding from the lower cognitive levels to the higher. She is processing information in more complex ways as the investigation continues. Such information should indicate her level of functioning regarding questions. If the profile indicated that after three weeks of considering the market place, she was still primarily posing knowledge questions, then the profile should alert her to that shortcoming. Most of the process models, whether inductive or deductive, require the student to go beyond the knowledge level and also to alter the questions as to cognitive level.

With regard to the affective domain, our student could focus on her questions that centered on the values she held regarding the free market or the values of individuals. When processing information at the analysis level, attention can be given to the affective level of valuing and organization. The nature of the plan suggested also would indicate the values an individual had incorporated into his or her value schema. Therefore, the profile of the affective domain should somewhat parallel the one indicated for the cognitive domain. Surely, a learner would not get into asking analysis and synthesis questions if at the same time he or she did not evidence a willingness to deal with the topic under consideration or to value somewhat the information being processed. Judgments relating to increasing market's efficiency would indicate clearly some of the value organization schema the learner possessed.

Assessing Activity 16: Environment Check

BASIC RATIONALE. The environment in which students discover themselves certainly either retards or facilitates their functioning. If students are to utilize various process models all involving the use of questions, they must discover if the environment provides those types of materials required for successful data processing. Are materials present that will suggest higher order questions, or are all materials secondary materials tending to lead learners to utilize lower levels of questions? Is the environment conducive to encounters with classmates to brainstorm questions potentially relevant to a particular topic? Are resource persons available in the school or in the immediate community environment with whom class members can interact?

Such questions need to be asked to critique the environment as to whether it encourages or retards positing questions at higher cognitive and affective levels. Of course, this environment check can be done prior to investigation, which could make it a planning activity, or it can be done after the students had worked with data.

THE ACTIVITY. Basically, the environment check consists of indicating aspects of the environment and then making some judgment about whether these aspects are facilitating or retarding questions. If they are facilitating, then this is good knowledge to possess; if they are inhibiting the learner's questions, awareness is a first step in modifying the environment to enable more effective questioning to take place.

Environment Check

TOPIC: _____

ENVIRONMENTAL FACTOR	FACILITATES GOOD QUESTIONS	RETARDS GOOD QUESTIONS

RECOMMENDATIONS:_____

_____

_____

_____

Example. For our example, students are engaged in the study of a health unit, specifically relating to the place of physical activity in life. The major objective of the unit is to determine just how physical activity facilitates basic health and to suggest ways to maintain such activity for continued good health. Since this activity is being considered as an assessment activity, the students are already involved in the unit study. Perhaps at the end of the first major segment of the unit they become concerned with whether the environment is providing them with the necessary kinds of support required for achieving the objective of the unit. The following chart indicates the work of an individual as he assesses the environment with regard to whether it is facilitating his questions.

Environment Check

TOPIC: Health, Physical Activity

ENVIRONMENTAL FACTOR	FACILITATES	RETARDS
Books	Facilitates questions at K and Comp levels	
Primary Sources, Lacking		Retards questions aimed at analysis.
Space		Retards working with peers to get questions aimed at coming to a conclusion
Multimedia Materials	Facilitate questions at upper levels but insufficient number relating to many aspects of the topic	

RECOMMENDATIONS: The class environment should provide for diversity of materials, books, primary sources of materials, and multimedia materials. I seem to ask better questions when I work with primary source materials. I have difficulty phrasing questions dealing with analysis when just reading the health books.

Note. Other learners may react differently to the various environmental factors. If the teacher obtains such information from the student, it will enable the teacher to be more effective in planning for meeting individual differences, in this case with regard to student question-asking behavior.

CONCLUDING NOTES

This chapter discussed activities relating to involving students in assessing their questions and the questions of others, whether in written or verbal form. The encounters represent means by which teachers can involve students in the assessment of their information processing.

It was pointed out that this assessment stage was not to be confused with evaluation of worth of learning outcomes. That is the final stage of learning, the determination of whether information gained or conclusions developed are warranted and useful. These activities are not concerned primarily with judging the worth of information gained, only with an inspection, as it were, of the process by which outputs are achieved.

There was not a definite sequence of activities presented for it is not possible to outline with precision what the teacher should have the student do first, second, or third. The sequence of the activities depends upon the learners and the nature of the actual inquiry. It should be reiterated that when using the activities in this book, the teacher should not do all of the planning activities, and then all of the doing activities, and finally the assessing activities. Rather, it would seem that the teacher would engage students with some of the planning activities, which would lead to some of the doing or involvement activities, which would conclude with some of the assessing activities. At various times, the teacher would involve the learners with different combinations of these three major stages. As already indicated, students should be privy to all of this information, and they can decide some of the sequences to suit their own needs.

7

Relating Questions to Models of Teaching, Modes of Discovery, and Other Points

INTRODUCTION

In the previous chapters, we have directed attention to means of involving individuals in planning, doing, and assessing their questions. The primary purpose of these activities is to enable students to comprehend questions to the degree necessary for optional information processing.

Questions, as has been pointed out several times, are central to learning and comprise the integral component of teaching and learning strategies. We can consider teaching-learning as an interacting dyad. In those situations where students assume the prime role for their learning by asking questions and processing information, they are really utilizing teaching models similar to, if not identical to, those employed by teachers.

There are several books on the market that deal with teaching models in detail. Joyce and Weil[1] have discussed models drawn from social interaction, information processing, discovery of self, and behavior modification. Models implied in the three chapters of planning, doing, and assessing focus primarily on schemes dealing with processing information, although prototypes dealing with the other models also are implied.

In introducing their section on information processing as a source of models, Joyce and Weil indicate that such models exist within realms of reference relating to how individuals process information and are derived from several sources:[2]

–from developmental studies of the intellectual capacity of the human being.

–from conceptualizations of mental processes.

–from learning theorists who have developed systems for enhancing particular kinds of information processing.

–from the *Syntactical Structures* of the scholarly disciplines, which may be seen as systems for processing information.

The activities that have been presented in the previous three chapters have drawn in part from all of these sources, but the activities primarily represent student involvement based on conceptualizations of mental processes and syntactical structures of the scholarly disciplines. The activities indicate two prime purposes of the school: assisting students in becoming knowledgeable about process and assisting students in utilizing process to obtain more complete understanding of the world of learning. This does not imply that the activities included in the text eliminate other goals such as creating effective self-concept or preparation for certain careers, but the school has to rank purposes. Also, one can argue that if students become effective processors of information and utilize their process skills to achieve better understanding of content, e.g. facts, concepts, generalizations, principles, theories, procedures, values, then other aims, such as facilitating the development of improved self-image, will be achieved as well.

INDUCTIVE-DEDUCTIVE MODES

Another way of contemplating models of teaching is to consider them within the frameworks of whether they are inductive or deductive. Some confusion exists as to these processes and oftentimes induction and deduction are used to indicate how individuals process information rather than a particular teaching method. In reality one cannot exclude either mental process or teaching strategy: inductive teaching strategies foster inductive student functioning, and deductive teaching strategies stimulate deductive student functioning.

In this text both induction and deduction are implied in the various activities discussed, and the terms are applicable to both teacher behavior in structuring lessons for student involvement as well as to the mental processes actually used by students. Regardless of the tack you take, it cannot be denied that the question is used in both induction and deduction.

Morine and Morine indicate several modes of discovery: open inductive discovery, structured inductive discovery, simple deductive discovery, semideductive discovery, hypotheticodeductive discovery, and transductive discovery.[3] The chart on page 224 delineates the major characteristics of these several modes.

The open inductive discovery lesson involves individuals primarily in the collection and reordering of data for the purpose of developing some new grouping of information as a category, a concept, or a generalization. As the chart shows, the major thrust of such a lesson is not upon individual discovery or any particular concept or generalization, but rather

Types of Discovery

DISCOVERY TYPE	TYPE OF STUDENT THINKING STRESSED	PRIME AIM	MANNER OF STUDENT FUNCTIONING
Open inductive	Inductive	Learning the process	Collection and reordering of data for practice in process
Structured inductive	Inductive	Acquiring specific understanding	Collecting data relating to specific subject matter
Deductive discovery	Deductive	To generate questions to formulate logical links among information	Responding to questions phrased by teacher
Semideductive discovery	Inductive	To learn concepts basic to a field of study	Learning concepts inductively and applying them to particular situations
Hypotheti-codeductive discovery	Deductive	To generate hypotheses as to cause and relationship To create tests for hypotheses advanced	Hypothesizing, predicting results Evaluating whether conclusions warranted
Transductive discovery	Transductive	To develop skill in creative thinking	Working with information in novel ways Comparing particular items for similar characteristics and arriving at unusual deductions

on student involvement with data in order to begin to comprehend the process itself. Such discovery aims at getting individuals to grasp how to learn in the sense of coming to organize data. Many of the activities in this book stress having students learn the process of utilizing questions in meaningful ways.

The structured inductive discovery mode aims at taking learners one step further from a realization of process to the actual utilization of process to gain a more complete understanding of some dimension of knowledge. Students are to utilize process in order to attain specific learnings, facts, concepts, generalizations, rules, and principles. Such discovery involves using questions to acquire specific understanding relating to particular subject matter. Throughout this text there are numerous activities that emphasize not just the learning of process, but its utilization in order to understand some information more completely.

The third type of discovery depicted in the chart, deductive discovery, is geared to having students generate questions which will lead to formulating logical links among information. The manner of student-teacher functioning resembles in part the Socratic method of questioning in which the teacher assumes the dominant role of utilizing questions to control the data the students confront and the directions of their responses. Questions used in this model "lead" students to particular conclusions. In this book there are some activities that can lead students to their own deductions and help them to synthesize specific conclusions within predetermined areas of investigation.

The fourth type of discovery, semideductive discovery, is utilized to get students to learn concepts inductively and then to utilize them deductively by applying the concepts to particular situations. The application of the concepts arrived at inductively to specific situations makes this a hybrid type of discovery.

Hypotheticodeductive discovery directs learners to generate hypotheses as to causes and relationships and then to

ideate means to test these hypotheses. This type of discovery
assumes that students are at the formal stage of cognitive
development. There are numerous activities in this textbook
which evidence this method of discovery in which students
use questions to generate various hypotheses for investigation
and then employ these questions to determine possible means
of verification. Considering questions and indicating probable directions of investigations also pertain to this type of
discovery.

The final type of discovery listed on the chart, transductive discovery, refers to what some might call intuitive
reasoning, the use of serendipity, intuitive leaps, creative
thinking. Specifically, it refers to methods to enable students
to process information in ways that might be considered non-
logical, but are definitely imaginative or creative. The use of
questions in this type of discovery stresses creativity: what
questions can the student pose that will allow analyzing a
situation or data in a different manner? Activities in which
students are asked to brainstorm types of possible questions
exemplify this type of discovery as well as lessons stressing
straight creativity.

SOME POINTS TO CONSIDER

A major assumption of this book is that the student is
capable of processing information and asking meaningful
questions. It has been maintained throughout this text that
the question is the germ of inquiry and the handle by which
students investigate information in order to obtain comprehensive insight into various realms of meaning. It should be
stressed that these activities are not just for gifted students.
If given time and guidance by the teacher the overwhelming
majority of students can comprehend the various types of
questions and the ways in which questions can be utilized to
process information.

This assumption relates to a change in view regarding the intellectual nature of man, a shift from a Newtonian consideration of man as one with a genetically fixed intelligence to an Einsteinian view of man as an individual possessing a modifiable intelligence. Barbara Blitz[4] maintains that to instruct this person requires an education conducive to active learner involvement. Educators with this view require a school with a richness of materials, environments, activities, situations, encounters, confrontations. In brief, such a school has an educational environment in which the learner can seek actively and ask questions, where he can chart his course somewhat and make corrections as they are required.

Notes for Prospective and In-Service Teachers

If the concept of school is being altered and the role of the student is being modified, then we as educators and teachers must assume different roles as well. The activities suggested in this book assume that we teachers can accept the roles of education manager, guide, stimulator, and catalyst as well as the more traditional roles of expositor and information giver. If school is to be a diverse and rich environment conducive to learning, then educators must become competent instructional and curriculum planners and implementors and creative managers of the educational environment.

Additionally, we will need to be effective diagnosticians and guides so that students can be involved optimally. The activities suggested in this book have learners planning their learning, positing questions, carrying out plans relating to their questioning, and diagnosing their successes relating to their questions. Such learner involvement requires competent educational and psychological support from us.

The crucial note for us as in-service or prospective teachers is that we must alter our primary role of "teller" of information to that of designer of situations in which students can process information, or specifically, work with questions. We educators must assume a legion of roles: question stimulator, question asker, guide, motivator, mediator, diagnostician, environment designer, catalyst, fellow student, evaluator, advocate, and friend.

CONCLUDING NOTES

The major purpose of this book is to furnish readers with activities designed to involve students in three dimensions of questioning: planning, using, and assessing. The book is designed to provide practical ideas about what teachers can do to get *all* students working with questions.

The activities suggested can be related to several models of teaching and numerous modes of discovery. This information is included to reveal some of the fields of educational investigation and thought that support the activities included in the book.

Without question, the emphasis of the text is on activities, but some attention is directed to the reasons for such concern with questions and questioning in the classroom as well as with types of questions at both cognitive and affective levels.

The major thrust of the book is on involvement, not teacher involvement in the usual sense, but student involvement. Of course, the teacher is involved in planning situations in which the students would become engaged in the activities suggested. The teacher will have to provide the necessary materials, the rich educational environment, the psychological support, the scheduling of adequate time. Also, the teacher will be engaged in providing guidance, motivation, and assessment of the effectiveness of his or her plans in creating situations for involving students.

Perhaps at no other time in history has the challenge to education been as great. The decisions we make regarding including students in their learning will have some immediate results; but others will not be discernible until some future time. The challenge to educators is to provide learners with competencies requisite for meeting the challenges of today and tomorrow and the commitment necessary for enacting those competencies in order that the world will become an even better place in which to exist. The stage is set.

NOTES

1. BRUCE JOYCE and MARSHA WEIL, *Models of Teaching* (Englewood Cliffs, N.J.: Prentice-Hall, Inc., 1972).

2. Ibid., p. 105.

3. HAROLD MORINE and GRETA MORINE, *Discovery, A Challenge to Teachers* (Englewood Cliffs, N.J.: Prentice-Hall, Inc., 1973), pp. 81-90.

4. BARBARA BLITZ, *The Open Classroom, Making It Work* (Boston: Allyn and Bacon, 1973), p. 5.

Appendix A

Research Studies Dealing with Questions and Questioning

Some of the major studies dealing with questions and questioning are listed. It is hoped that the reader will refer to some of these studies to augment his or her understanding of and commitment to this realm of knowledge.

ADAMS, T. H. "The Development of a Method for Analysis of Questions Asked by Teachers in Classroom Discourse." Unpublished doctoral dissertation, Rutgers University, 1964.

ASCHWALD, H. G. "Some Relationships Between Teacher Cognitive Verbal Behavior and Student Cognitive Verbal Response in Secondary Social Studies Classes." Unpublished doctoral dissertation, University of Oregon, 1969.

BOONE, S. M. "An Investigation of the Effects of Higher Level Questions on Reading Comprehension." Unpublished doctoral dissertation, University of Washington, 1971.

BUGGEY, L. J. "A Study of the Relationship of Classroom Questions and Social Studies Achievement of Secondary Grade

Children." Unpublished doctoral dissertation, University of Washington, 1971.

CLEGG, A. A., G. T. FARLEY, and R. J. CURRAN. "Training Teachers to Analyze the Cognitive Level of Classroom Questioning." Research Report No. 1, Applied Research Training Program, University of Massachusetts, 1967.

CORNELL, E. F. "Observational Learning of Question-Asking Behavior Through the Medium of Audio-Tapes." Unpublished doctoral dissertation, University of Maryland, 1969.

CRUMP, C. D. "Self-Instruction in the Art of Questioning in Intermediate-Grade Social Studies." Unpublished doctoral dissertation, Indiana University, 1969.

CUNNINGHAM, R. T. "A Descriptive Study Determining the Effects of a Method of Instruction Designed to Improve the Question-Phrasing Practices of Prospective Elementary Teachers." Unpublished doctoral dissertation, University of Oregon, 1969.

DAHLBERG, E. J. "An Analysis of the Relationships Between the Cognitive Level of Teacher Questions and Selected Variables." Unpublished doctoral dissertation, University of Oregon, 1969.

DAVIS, O. L., Jr. and F. P. HUNKINS. "Textbook Questions: What Thinking Processes Do They Foster?" *Peabody Journal of Education* 43 (March 1966): 285-92.

DAVIS, O. L. and K. R. MORSE. "The Effectiveness of Teaching Laboratory Instruction on the Questioning Behavior of Beginning Teacher Candidates." Report Series No. 43, The Research and Development Center for Teacher Education, The University of Texas at Austin, 1970 (ED 037 384).

DAVIS, O. L. and K. R. MORSE. "The Questioning Strategies Observation System." Report Series No. 35, The Research and Development Center for Teacher Education, The University of Texas at Austin, 1970.

DAVIS, O. L. and D. C. TINSLEY. "Cognitive Objectives Revealed by Classroom Questions Asked by Social Studies Student Teachers." *Peabody Journal of Education* 45 (July, 1967): 21-26.

DOUCE, H. L. "Raising the Cognitive Level of Teacher Questioning Behavior in Selected Schools." Unpublished doctoral dissertation, University of Washington, 1971.

FARLEY, G. T. "Increasing the Cognitive Level of Classroom Questions: An Application of Bloom's *Taxonomy of Educational Objectives.*" Unpublished doctoral dissertation, University of Massachusetts, 1968.

FLOYD, W. D. "An Analysis of the Oral Questioning Activity in Selected Colorado Primary Classrooms." Unpublished doctoral dissertation, Colorado State University, 1960.

FRASE, L. T. "Effective Prose Reading: Shaping and Discriminative Effects of Questions." Paper read at the Annual Convention of the American Educational Research Association, Chicago, February 1968.

_____. "Learning from Prose Material: Length of Passage, Knowledge of Results and Position of Questions." *Journal of Educational Psychology* 58 (1967): 266-72.

GUSZAK, F. J. "Questioning Strategies of Elementary Teachers in Relation to Comprehension." Paper presented at the International Reading Association Conference, Boston, April, 1968.

HUNKINS, F. P. "The Influence of Analysis and Evaluation Questions on Achievement and Critical Thinking in Sixth Grade Social Studies," U.S. Department of Health, Education, and Welfare, Final Report, Cooperative Research Project, 1968.

_____. "The Influence of Analysis and Evaluation Questions on Achievement in Sixth Grade Social Studies." *Educational Leadership* (Research Supplement) January 1968.

_____. "The Effects of Analysis and Evaluation Questions on Various Levels of Achievement." *Journal of Experimental Education* 38 (Winter 1969): 45-58.

_____. "Analysis and Evaluation Questions: Their Effects Upon Critical Thinking." *Educational Leadership* (Research Supplement) April 1970.

JOHNS, J. P. "Relationship Between Teacher Behaviors and the Incidence of Thought-Provoking Questions by Students in Secondary Schools." *Journal of Educational Research* 62 (November 1968): 117-122.

JOHNSON, C. L. "The Effect of Higher-Cognitive Questioning Skill Training on the Questioning Practices of Pre-Service, Intermediate Grade School Teachers." Unpublished doctoral dissertation, University of Oregon, 1971.

JOHNSON, J. R. "The Acquisition of Questioning Skills Among Pre-Service Elementary Social Studies Teachers Through a Self-Directed Learning Experience." Unpublished doctoral dissertation, The Pennsylvania State University, 1972.

KLEINMAN, G. "Teachers' Questions and Student Understanding of Science." *Journal of Research in Science Teaching* 3 (December, 1965): 307-317.

LADD, G. T. "Determining the Level of Inquiry in Teachers' Questions." Unpublished doctoral dissertation, Indiana University, 1969.

MANSON, G. A. "The Effects of Immediate and Postponed Observer Feedback on the Acquisition of Higher Order Questioning Skills by Prospective Teachers." Unpublished doctoral dissertation, The University of Washington, 1970.

MITTELSTADT, J. W. "The Description and Analysis of Questioning Strategies of Elementary Education Student Teachers Prior to and Following the Implementation of an Inquiry Observation Instrument." Unpublished doctoral dissertation, Wayne State University, 1969.

MONROE, W. S. and R. E. CARTER. "The Use of Different Types of Thought Questions in Secondary Schools and Their Relationship to Difficulty for Students." *Bureau of Educational Research Bulletin.* Urbana: University of Illinois, 1923.

MOYER, J. R. "An Exploratory Study of Questioning in the Instructional Processes in Selected Elementary Schools." Unpublished doctoral dissertation, Columbia University, 1965.

PORTERFIELD, D. R. "Influence of Preparation in Science Curriculum Improvement Study on Questioning Behavior of Selected Second and Fourth Grade Reading Teachers." Unpublished doctoral dissertation, The University of Oklahoma, 1969.

PSENCIK, L. F. "Some Relationships Between Attitude, Verbal Behavior, and Cognitive Level of Classroom Questions of Secondary American History." Unpublished doctoral dissertation, Texas A & M University, 1971.

QUIRING, J. D. "The Effects of Questioning Level and Feedback Timing on the Achievement of Sophomore Nursing Students Using an Auto-Tutorial Approach." Unpublished doctoral dissertation, University of Washington, 1971.

RICKARDS, J. P. and F. J. DI VESTA. "Type and Frequency of Questions in Processing Textual Material." *Journal of Educational Psychology* 66 (1974): 354-362.

ROGERS, V. A. "Varying the Cognitive Levels of Classroom Questions in Elementary Social Studies: An Analysis of the Use of Questions by Student Teachers." Unpublished doctoral dissertation, University of Texas at Austin, 1969.

ROTHKOPH, E. A. and E. E. BISBICOS. "Selective Facilitative Effects of Interspersed Questions on Learning From Written Materials." *Journal of Educational Psychology* 58 (1967): 56-61.

SAVAGE, T. V. "A Study of the Relationship of Classroom Questions and Social Studies Achievement of Fifth-Grade Children." Unpublished doctoral dissertation, University of Washington, 1972.

SCHREIBER, J. E. "Teacher's Question-Asking Techniques in Social Studies." Unpublished doctoral dissertation, University of Iowa, 1967.

STEVENS, R. "The Question as a Measure of Efficiency in Instruction: A Critical Study of Classroom Practice." *Teachers College Contributions to Education* (New York: Columbia University Press, 1912).

TINSLEY, D. C. "A Study in Planning: Questions to Guide Discussion and Testing by Secondary Student Teachers of Social Studies." Unpublished doctoral dissertation, The University of Texas at Austin, 1968.

TYLER, J. F. "A Study of the Relationship of Two Methods of Questioning Presentation, Sex and School Location to the Social Studies Achievement of Second Grade Children." Unpublished doctoral dissertation, University of Washington, 1971.

WADSWORTH, B. and B. FLAGG, "The Effect of Interspersed Questions on Learning from Written Materials in Elementary School Children and College Students." Paper presented at the Annual Convention of the American Educational Research Association, New York, 1971.

WILEN, W. W. "The Preferences of American History Students for the Cognitive Levels of Teachers' Verbal Questioning Behavior and the Relationship of Preferences to Achievement." Unpublished doctoral dissertation, The Pennsylvania State University, 1973.

ZOCH, F. R. "The Effect of an Individualized In-Service Program on Teacher Questioning and Student Verbal Participation." Unpublished doctoral dissertation, University of Houston, 1970.

Appendix B

Reviews of Studies
on Questions
and Questioning

The following reviews can be utilized to gain an overall view of research activity in the realm of questions and questioning.

CLEGG, A. A., Jr., "Classroom Questions," in Lee C. Deighton, ed. *The Encyclopedia of Education*, vol. 2. (New York: Macmillan, 1971).

DAVIS, O. L., K. R. MORSE, V. M. ROGERS, and D. C. TINSLEY. "Studying the Cognitive Emphasis of Teachers' Classroom Questions." *Educational Leadership* 26 (April, 1969): 711-719.

GALL, M. D. "The Use of Questions in Teaching," *Review of Educational Research* 40 (1970): 707-721.

Index

236